By Oriana Fallaci

Oriana Fallaci

THE RAGE
AND
THE PRIDE

RIZZOLI
NEW YORK

Published by Rizzoli International Publications, Inc.
300 Park Avenue South
New York, NY 10010

Library of Congress Catalog Control Number: 2002112059

ISBN-13: 978-0-8478-2504-2

Original Title: La Rabbia e l'Orgoglio

Copyright © 2001 RCS Libri SpA
First published in the United States of America in 2002
by Rizzoli International Publications, Inc.
300 Park Avenue South
New York, NY 10010

Printed in Italy

First edition: September 2002
Second edition: November 2002
Third edition: December 2002
Fourth edition: February 2003
Fifth edition: March 2006
Sixth edition: January 2007

2007 2008 2009 / 11 10 9 8 7 6

To my parents, Edoardo and Tosca Fallaci,
who taught me to tell the truth
and to my uncle, Bruno Fallaci,
who taught me how to write it.

To *the* *English-speaking reader*

The translation of this book is mine.
Although it has been somewhat revised,
it still contains what my critics define as
"the oddities of Fallaci's English".
Meaning, a punctuation and a lexical choice
and above all a construction of the phrase
which reflects or repeats my way
of writing in Italian: my language.
Though I recognize that some mistakes
may accompany those "oddities", I offer it as it is.
The translation is mine and I choose
to offer it as it is because,
given the importance of what I tell, given
the gravity of what I maintain,
I want to have total responsibility
for every word and comma I publish
under my name in this language
that I love as much as my own.

Oriana Fallaci

PREFACE

I had chosen silence. I had chosen exile. Because, the time has come to say it loud and clear, in America I live as a political refugee. I mean, in the political self-exile that both my father and I imposed on ourselves when we realized that living in a country where the ideals lay in the garbage had become too painful, too difficult, and disillusioned wounded offended we burnt the bridges with the great majority of our compatriots. My father, retiring to a remote hill of Chianti where the politics to which he had dedicated his life as a noble and upright man did not reach him. I, roving around the world then stopping in New York where between me and those compatriots there was the Atlantic Ocean. Such parallelism may seem bizarre, I know. But when exile lodges inside a disillusioned and wounded and offended soul, the geographical collocation does not matter: believe me. When you love your country, when because of your country you suffer, there is no difference between living as a writer in a metropolis of ten million inhabitants and living as a Cincinnatus on a remote hill of Chianti with your dogs and your cats and your chickens. The solitude is identical. So is the sense of defeat.

Besides, New York has always been a haven for political refugees, political exiles. In 1850, after the fall of the Roman Republic and the death of Anita and the flight from Italy, even Giuseppe Garibaldi came here: remember? He arrived the 30th of July on a ship from Liverpool, so bitterly hurt that the first thing he said while descending the ramp was «I-want-to-ask-for-the-American-citizenship», and during the first two months he lived as a guest of the Leghorn merchant Pastacaldi in Manhattan: 26 Irving Place. (An address I know very well because it was there that eleven years later my great-grandmother Anastasìa, in her turn a fugitive from Italy, took shelter). Then, in October, he moved to Staten Island as a guest of Antonio Meucci: the ingenious Florentine who invented the telephone but, not having the money to renew the patent, saw his precious idea taken away by a guy named Alexander Bell... Here along with Meucci he opened a sausage workshop which for lack of success had to be soon transformed into a candle factory, and in the tavern where every Sa-

turday night both of them used to play cards (the *Ventura Tavern on Fulton Street*) he once left a note that read: «*Damn the sausages, bless the candles, God save Italy if he can*». But, before Garibaldi, guess who came. In 1833, Piero Maroncelli: the patriot who at the Spielberg penitentiary had been in the same cell with Silvio Pellico, and who in New York would die thirteen years later of poverty and nostalgia. In 1835, Federico Confalonieri: the patriot whom the Austrians had condemned to death but whom Teresa Casati (his wife) had saved by throwing herself at the feet of the Emperor of Austria. In 1836, Felice Foresti: the patriot whose death penalty had been commuted by the Austrians to life imprisonment then to fourteen years. In 1837, the twelve Lombards who had been condemned to the gallows but whom the Austrians (always more civil than the Pope and the Bourbons, let's admit it) had pardoned. In 1838, the indomitable general Giuseppe Avezzana who by default had been condemned to death for participating in the first Piedmont constitutional movement...

Nor is this all. Because many others came after Garibaldi: remember? In 1858, for instance, the historian Vincenzo Botta who soon became Professor Emeritus at New York University. And at the beginning of the Civil War, the 28th of May

1861 to be exact, it was right here in New York that our Garibaldi Guards arrived and formed the Thirty-Ninth N.Y. Infantry Regiment. Yes, the legendary Garibaldi Guards who along with the American flag carried the Italian flag with which they had fought since 1848 for their country, and on which they had written the motto «Vincere o Morire - Victory or Death». The famous Thirty-Ninth N.Y. Infantry Regiment that the following week Lincoln reviewed in Washington and that during the following years distinguished itself in the bloody battles of First Bull Run, Cross Keys, Gettysburg, North Anna, Bristoe Station, Po River, Mine Run, Spotsylvania, Wilderness, Cold Harbor, Strawberry Plain, Petersburg, Deep Bottom Creek, until Appomattox. If you don't believe it, look at the obelisk which stands at Cemetery Ridge (Gettysburg) and read the inscription commemorating the Italians killed the 2nd of July 1863: the day when they recaptured the cannons taken by the Fifth U.S. Artillery Regiment of General Lee. «Passed away before life's noon / Who shall say they died too soon? / Ye who mourn, oh, cease from tears / Deeds like these outlast the years».

As for the political refugees who found asylum in New York during Fascism, well: they were even more numerous. And as a little girl I knew most of them because like my father they

14

belonged to «Justice and Liberty»: the movement built up by Carlo and Nello Rosselli before being assassinated in France by Mussolini's French mercenaries. I mean, by the Cagoulards. In 1924, Girolamo Valenti who founded the New York antifascist paper «The New World». In 1925, Armando Borghi who established the «Italo-American Resistance». In 1926, Carlo Tresca and Arturo Giovannitti who created «The Antifascist Alliance of North America». In 1927, the extraordinary Gaetano Salvemini who soon moved to Cambridge to teach History at Harvard University but all the same traveled throughout the States deafening Americans with his lectures against Hitler and Mussolini. (In my living room I keep the poster of one. I keep it in a fine silver frame and it reads: «Sunday May 7, 1933, at 2:30 p.m., Antifascist Meeting at the Irving Plaza Hotel. Irving Plaza and 15th Street, New York City. Professor G. Salvemini, Internationally-known Historian, will speak on Hitler and Mussolini. The meeting will be held under the auspices of the Italian organization Justice and Liberty. Admission, 25 cents»). In 1931, Arturo Toscanini (his great friend) who had just been cudgeled in Bologna by the father of the future son-in-law of Mussolini, Costanzo Ciano, for refusing to perform in one of his concerts the Black Shirts' anthem «Youth, Youth, Spring of Beauty». In 1940

15

Alberto Tarchiani, Alberto Cianca, Aldo Garosci, Max Ascoli, Nicola Chiaromonte, Emilio Lussu: the antifascist intellectuals who gave birth to the «Mazzini Society» and to the monthly magazine «United Nations»...

I mean: here I am in good company. When I miss the Italy which is not the unhealthy Italy I referred to at the beginning, (and I always miss her), I only have to call those noble models of my childhood: to smoke a cigarette with them and ask them for consolation. «Give me a hand, professor Salvemini. Cheer me up, professor Cianca. Help me to forget, professor Garosci». Or else, to invoke the glorious ghosts of Garibaldi, Maroncelli, Confalonieri, Foresti, Avezzana, etc. To bow in front of them, offer them a brandy, play for them the record with the chorus of «Nabucco» performed by the Philharmonic Orchestra of New York and directed by Arturo Toscanini. And when I miss Florence, when I miss my Tuscany, (something that happens even more often), I only have to jump on a plane and fly home. Stealthily, though. That is, like Giuseppe Mazzini did when he stealthily left his London exile to reach Turin and visit his beloved Giuditta Sidoli... In Florence and Tuscany, in fact, I live much more than people believe. Often, months and months in a row or a year at a time. If nobody knows, it is because I co-

me in the Mazzini way. And if I come in the Mazzini way, it is because it repulses me to meet the thugs for whose thuggishness my father died in self-exile on the remote hill of Chianti and I risk dying here in the same way.

Well, exile requires discipline and coherency. Virtues in which I have been educated by two first-rate parents. A father who had the strength of a Gaius Mucius Scaevola, a mother who resembled Cornelia the Mother of the Gracchi, and who (both of them) considered severity an antidote against irresponsibility.** And out of discipline, out of coherence, in these years I have remained as silent as an old and disdainful wolf. A wolf that consumes itself in the desire to sink its fangs into the sheep's throat, the rabbits' neck, yet succeeds in maintaining control. But there are moments in Life when keeping silent becomes a fault, and speaking an obligation. A civic duty, a moral challenge,

** *Author's note.* Gaius Mucius Scaevola is the Roman hero (Sixth Century B.C.) who stoically burnt his right hand to punish himself for the mistake of having killed a common soldier instead of King Porsenna: the Etruscan enemy who was keeping Rome under siege. Cornelia (Second Century B.C.) is the bold Roman matron who refused the throne of Egypt to dedicate herself to the education of her twelve children, the Gracchi, and teach them the principles of democracy.

a categorical imperative from which we cannot escape. Thus, eighteen days after the New York apocalypse, I broke my silence with the long article I published in the major Italian newspaper then in some foreign magazines. And now I interrupt (I do not break, I interrupt) my exile with this small-book which doubles the text of that article. I must therefore explain why it doubles it, how it doubles it, and in what way this small-book was born.

*   *   *

It was born all of a sudden. It burst like a bomb. Unexpectedly like the catastrophe that on September 11 disintegrated thousands of creatures and destroyed two of the most beautiful buildings of our time: the Towers of the World Trade Center. The eve of the apocalypse I was concentrating on something quite different: the book I call my-child. A massive and engaging novel that during these years I have never abandoned, that at most I have left for a few weeks or a few months to get treatment in some hospital or to conduct in some archive the research it is based upon. A very difficult, very demanding child whose gestation has lasted a great part of my adult life, whose delivery has begun thanks to the illness that will kill me, and whose first whimper will be heard I don't know when.

Maybe when I am dead. (Why not? Posthumous works have the exquisite advantage of saving the author's eyes and ears from the imbecilities or the perfidiousness of those who, not being capable of writing and not even conceiving a novel, have the pretense to judge and abuse those who conceive it and write it). Yes: the morning of September 11 I was so involved with my-child, that in order to overcome the trauma I said to myself: «I must not think of what has happened and is happening. I must take care of my baby and that's all. Otherwise it ends with a miscarriage». Then, clenching my teeth, I sat down at the desk. I tried to concentrate on the page written the day before, to carry my mind back to the novel's characters. All characters of a remote world, of a time when airplanes and skyscrapers certainly did not exist. But it did not last. The smell of death came from the windows along with the obsessive sounds of police-cars, of fire-trucks, of ambulances, of helicopters, of military jets flying over the city. The TV set (that because of the anguish I had left on) kept blinking with the images I wanted to forget... Suddenly I walked out. I looked for a taxi, I did not find it, by foot I directed myself toward the Towers that no longer existed, and...

Afterwards, I did not know what to do. In what way to make myself useful, to be of some service. And just while I was asking myself what-

do-I-do, what-can-I-do, the TV displayed the Pale-
stinians who rejoiced and applauded over the mas-
sacre. They cheered, they repeated Victory-Victory.
Almost at the same time a friend came and told me
that in Europe, Italy included, many imitated them
sneering «Good. Americans got it good». Therefo-
re, like a soldier who jumps out of the trench and
launches himself against the enemy, I jumped on
my typewriter and started doing the only thing
I could do: write. Twitch notes, at times. Disordered
memos that I took for myself. Concepts, remem-
brances, invectives that from America flew to Eu-
rope. Or should I say to Italy. From Italy, to the Mo-
slem countries. From the Moslem countries, back
to America. Ideas that for years I had imprisoned
inside my heart and my brain, saying to myself:
«Why bother? What for? People are deaf. They
don't listen, don't want to listen...». Now they gu-
shed out of me like a waterfall, those ideas. They
dropped on the paper as an unrestrainable cry. Be-
cause, you see, with tears I do not cry. Even if a
physical pain stabs me, even if an unbearable sor-
row lacerates me, tears do not well up in my eyes.
It's a sort of neurological dysfunction, or rather a
physiological mutilation that I have been carrying
within me for more than half a century. I mean,
since the 25th of September 1943. The Saturday
when the Allies bombarded Florence for the first

20

time and made a lot of mistakes. Instead of hitting the target, the railway that the Germans used to transport weapons and troops, they hit the nearby district and the historic cemetery of Donatello Square. The British Cemetery, the one where Elizabeth Barrett Browning is buried. I was with my father near the church of Santissima Annunziata that from Donatello Square is not even nine hundred feet away, when the bombs began to shower. To escape them we took refuge in the church, and how could I know the horror of a bombardment? At every bomb the solid walls of Santissima Annunziata oscillated like trees assailed by the tempest, the windows broke, the floor jolted, the altar wavered, the priest yelled «Jesus! Help us, Jesus!». And, all of a sudden, I started crying. In a silent, composed way, mind you. No moans, no hiccups. But Father noticed it all the same and in order to help me, to calm me down, poor father, did the wrong thing. He gave me a powerful slap, he stared me in the eyes and said: «A girl does not, must not, cry». So, since the 25th of September 1943, I do not cry. Thank God if sometimes my eyes get damp and my throat chokes a little. Inside myself, however, I cry more than those who cry with tears. Rather often, the words I write are nothing but tears. And what I wrote after the 11th of September was in reality an unrestrainable cry. Over the ali-

ve, over the dead. Over those who seem alive and instead are dead. Dead because they have no balls to change, to become people worthy of respect. And also over myself who, in the last phase of my life, must explain why in America I stay as a political refugee and in Italy I come by stealth.

Then, (I had been crying like that for six days), the editor-in-chief of the major Italian newspaper came to New York. He came to ask me to break the silence I had already broken. And I told him so. I even showed him the twitch notes, the disordered memos, but immediately he caught fire as if he had seen Greta Garbo throwing off her black glasses and parading in a licentious striptease on the stage of La Scala. Or as if he had seen my readers already lining up to buy the newspaper, pardon, to crowd into the stalls and the boxes and the gallery of the theater. All ablaze he asked me to go on, to sew the various pieces together with asterisks, to build up a sort of letter addressed to him, to send it as soon as completed. And driven by the civic duty, the moral challenge, the categorical imperative, I accepted. Again neglecting my-child now sleeping under those notes I returned to the typewriter where the unrestrainable cry became, rather than a letter, a scream of rage and pride. A J'accuse. A prosecution or a sermon addressed to the Europeans who, throwing me some flowers *maybe, but certainly many rotten eggs, would listen to me from the stalls and the boxes and the gallery of his newspaper. I worked another twelve days or so... Without stopping, without eating, without sleeping. I didn't even feel hungry or sleepy. I fed on coffee and that's all, I stayed awake with cigarettes and that's all. Without surrendering to fatigue, in short. But here I must point out something. I must say that writing is a very serious matter for me: it is not an amusement or an outlet or a relief. It is not because I never forget that written words can do a lot of good but also a lot of evil, they can heal as much as kill. Read History and you'll see that behind every event of Good or Evil there is a piece of writing. A book, an article, a manifesto, a poem, a song. (A Mameli Hymn, for example. A Marseillaise, a Yankee Doodle Dandy. Or a Bible, a Koran, a Das Kapital). So I never write rapidly, I never cast away: I am a slow writer, a cautious writer. I'm also an unappeasable writer: I do not resemble those who are always satisfied with their product as if they urinated ambrosia. Moreover I have many manias. I care for the rhythm of the phrase, for the cadence of the page, for the sound of the words: the metrics. And woe betide the assonances, the rhymes, the unwanted repetitions. For me the form is important as much as the substance, the content. It is the recipient in-*

side which the substance rests like wine inside a glass, like flour inside a jar, and managing such symbiosis at times blocks my work. This time, though, it did not. I wrote quickly, without worrying about the assonances and the rhymes and the repetitions because the metrics flourished by itself, and yet never forgetting that written words may heal as well as kill. (Can passion go so far?). The fact is that when I stopped, when I was ready to send the text, I realized that instead of an article I had given birth to a small-book. And to reduce it, to obtain a reasonable length, I shortened it by half. I cut the part on the two Buddhas slaughtered at Bamiyan, for instance. The one on the Cavaliere who governs Italy, the one on Alì Bhutto forced to get married at thirteen... Then I slipped them into a red folder, I put them to sleep with my-child. Yards and yards of papers on which I had spilled my heart. But in spite of those cuts the text turned out to be tremendously long. The ablaze editor-in-chief tried to help me. The two pages he had reserved in the newspaper became three then four then four and a quarter. A size never before reached, I believe, by a daily newspaper. He even proposed to publish it in two parts. Which I refused because in publishing it in two parts I would not have achieved what I intended. That is, trying to open the eyes of those who do not want to see, to unplug the ears of those *who do not want to listen, to ignite the thoughts of those who do not want to think. As a consequence, I shortened it even more. I set aside the most violent paragraphs, I streamlined the most complicated ones. Not feeling regrets, I confess. Because in the red folder I had those yards and yards of written papers. The complete text, the small-book.*

Well, the pages that follow this preface are the small-book. The complete text I wrote in the two or three weeks when I did not eat, I did not sleep, I fed on coffee, I kept awake with cigarettes, and the words fell on the paper like a waterfall. The corrections are few. (For instance the one about the 15.670 liras' discharge I received from the Italian Army when fourteen years old. And which in the newspaper had become a little less: 14.540). The additions are numerous, instead, and almost always concern the nazifascism that Islamic Fundamentalists epitomize with their behavior wherever they lodge... In a revolting and ungrammatical booklet entitled «Islam punishes Oriana Fallaci» now distributed in all the Moslem communities of Italy, for example, the so-called Italian Islamic Party's president (by the way an individual well known to the anti-terrorism police of Italy) has outrageously insulted my dead father and demanded his co-religionists to kill me in the name of Allah. «Go and die with Fallaci». In a trial

25

which has raised in Europe a considerable scandal because it has offended the first principle of every democratic society, the principle concerning the Freedom of Thought, an ultra-leftist Moslem association of Paris has tried to silence me by asking a French Court to confiscate «La Rage et l'Orgueil» or to label the jacket of each copy with a warning like the one that labels the cigarettes' packages. «Attention! The content of this volume may be hazardous to your health». Well... The French Court has rejected the request, I have won, but the association wants another trial and similar actions are taking place in other European countries. The revolting and ungrammatical booklet's author has got my lawsuit for slander and instigation to murder, and the anti-terrorism police has put him under control. But no day passes by without my receiving a threat from his brothers, and my life is seriously in danger.

* * *

I don't know if some day this small-book will grow even more and give me more troubles than it has given me till today. But I do know that in publishing it I feel as if I were Salvemini who on the 7th of May 1933 speaks at the Irving Plaza

against Hitler and Mussolini, shouting in despair addresses an audience that does not understand but will understand on the 7th of December 1941 (that is when the Japanese allied with Hitler and Mussolini will bomb Pearl Harbor) and implacably yells: «If you stay inert, if you don't lend us a hand, sooner or later they will attack you too!».
However there is a difference between my smallbook and Salvemini's 1933 speech. About Hitler and Mussolini, in fact, at that time Americans did not know what we Europeans knew and suffered. I mean the birth of nazifascism. They consequently could afford the luxury of not believing that political refugee who shouting in despair announced misfortunes for America too. About Islamic Fundamentalists, on the contrary, we Europeans know everything. Not even two months after the New York apocalypse, remember, Bin Laden himself proved that I am right when I shout: «You don't understand, you don't want to understand, that a Reverse Crusade is underway. A war of religion they call Holy War, Jihad. You don't understand, you don't want to understand, that for those Reverse Crusaders the West is a world to conquer and subjugate to Islam». He proved it with the video where he threatened even the United Nations and defined its Secretary General, Kofi Annan, «a criminal». The video in which he extended his

threats to the French, to the Italians, to the British, and which only lacked the hysterical voices of Hitler or Mussolini. The staging of Palazzo Venezia or the scenario of Alexanderplatz. «In its essence this is a war of religion and those who deny it are liars» he said. «All the Arabs and all the Moslems must draw up and fight, those who stay neutral disown Allah» he said. «The Arab and Moslem leaders who sit at the United Nations and share its politics place themselves outside Islam. They are Unfaithful, they do not respect the message of the Prophet» he said. And then: «Those who claim the legitimacy of international institutions give up the only authentic legitimacy, the legitimacy which comes from the Koran». And finally: «The overwhelming majority of the Moslems have been happy with the attacks on the Twin Towers. Our polls confirm it».

But was it really necessary to have his confirmation? From Afghanistan to Sudan, from Palestine to Pakistan, from Malaysia to Iran, from Egypt to Iraq, from Algeria to Senegal, from Syria to Kenya, from Libya to Chad, from Lebanon to Morocco, from Indonesia to Yemen, from Saudi Arabia to Somalia, the hate for the West swells like a fire fed by the wind. And the followers of Islamic Fundamentalism multiply like protozoa of a cell which splits to become two cells then four

28

then eight then sixteen then thirty-two to infinity.
Those who are not aware of it have only to look at
the images that TV brings us every day. The multi-
tudes that impregnate the streets of Islamabad, the
squares of Nairobi, the mosques of Tehran. The fe-
rocious faces, the threatening fists. The fires that
burn the American flag and the photos of Bush. He
or she who doesn't believe it has only to listen to
the hosannas to the Merciful-and-Wrathful God
that those multitudes invoke. Their yells Allah-
akbar, Allah-akbar. Jihad-Jihad... Extremist frin-
ges?!? Fanatical minorities?!? They are millions
and millions, the extremists. They are millions and
millions, the fanatics. The millions and millions
for whom, dead or alive, Ousama Bin Laden is a le-
gend similar to the legend of Khomeini. The mil-
lions and millions who after Khomeini's death
have chosen Bin Laden as their new leader, their
new hero. Last night I saw those of Nairobi, a place
about which we never talk. They filled the square
more than in Gaza or in Islamabad or Djakar-
ta, and a TV reporter interviewed an old man. He
asked him: «Who is, for you, Ousama Bin Laden?»
«A hero, our hero!» the old man joyfully answe-
red. «And what happens if he dies?» the TV repor-
ter added. «We find another one» the old man an-
swered, still joyfully. In other words, the one who
guides them is only the tip of the iceberg: the part

of the mountain which emerges from the abyss. Thus, the real protagonist of this war is not Bin Laden. Even less it is the country that hosts him or the country that gave him birth. I mean Saudi Arabia and supporters like Iran or Iraq or Syria or Palestine. It is the Mountain. That Mountain which in one thousand and four hundred years has not moved, has not risen from the abyss of its blindness, has not opened its doors to the conquests of civilization, has never wanted to know about freedom and democracy and progress. In short, has not changed. That Mountain which in spite of the shameful richness of its retrograde masters (kings and princes and sheiks and bankers) still lives in a scandalous poverty, still vegetates in the monstrous darkness of a religion which produces nothing but religion. That Mountain which drowns into illiteracy (don't forget that in almost every Moslem country the percentage of illiteracy surpasses sixty percent). That Mountain which gets information only through the backward Imams or the cartoon-strips. That Mountain which, secretly envious of us, unconfessedly jealous of our way of life, throws upon us the responsibility of its material and intellectual miseries. Wrong is he or she who believes that the Holy War has finished in 2001 with the disintegration of the Taliban regime in Afghanistan. Wrong is he or she who rejoices over the ima-

ges of Kabul women no longer wearing the burkah and finally going to school or to the doctor or to the hairdresser. Wrong is he or she who feels avenged in seeing Kabul men removing their beards like the Italians removed their fascist badges after the fall of Mussolini...

He is wrong, she is wrong, because beards grow again and burkahs can be put back on: over the last twenty years Afghanistan has been a continuous alternation of cut and regrown beards, a continuous taking off and putting back on the burkah. He is wrong, she is wrong, because the present winners or so-called winners pray to Allah as much as the defeated ones. And because from the defeated ones they distinguish themselves only for the length of the beards. In fact Afghan women are afraid of them as much as they were of their predecessors and do bear the same humiliations, the same iniquities, they bore with the Taliban. (At thirteen a girl can no longer dream of going to school, of walking in the streets, of sitting under a tree, don't forget). He is wrong, she is wrong, because the present winners fight one another as usual, nourish as usual the chaos, and because among the nineteen kamikazes of New York and Washington there was not a single Afghan. Besides, kamikazes have other places in which to train, other caves in which to hide. Look at the map and you'll see that south

of Afghanistan there is Pakistan. North of Afgha-
nistan, the Moslem Chechnya and Uzbekistan and
Kazakhstan, etc. West of Afghanistan, Iran. Next
to Iran, Iraq. Next to Iraq, Syria. Next to Syria, the
almost all-Moslem Lebanon. Next to Lebanon, the
Moslem Jordan. Next to Jordan, the ultra-Moslem
Saudi Arabia. And beyond the Red Sea there is the
African continent with its Moslem Egypt, Libya,
Somalia, Niger, Nigeria, Senegal, Mauritania etc,
its people who applaud the Holy War. Wrong, fi-
nally, because the clash between us and them is not
a military clash. Oh, no. It is a cultural one, a reli-
gious one. And our military victories do not solve
the offensive of Islamic terrorism. On the contrary,
they encourage it. They exacerbate it, they mul-
tiply it. The worst is still to come. Here is the bit-
ter truth. And Truth does not necessarily stay in
the middle. Sometimes it stays on one side only. At
the Irving Plaza meeting Salvemini too tried to
point out this fact that nobody accepts.

*　　*　　*

There is still another difference, however,
between this small-book and Salvemini's speech at
the Irving Plaza. Because the Americans who on
the 7th of May 1933 listened to his desperate shou-

ting did not have Hitler's SS or Mussolini's Black Shirts in their country. To deviate them from our reality, to enlarge their incredulousness, there was an ocean of water and a wall of isolationism. Nowadays, on the contrary, both Americans and Europeans have the various Bin Ladens' SS and Black Shirts on their soil. A soil where those SS and Black Shirts live unfeared, thus undisturbed. In America, thanks to an inflexible respect for every religion: one of the principles on which she was born. In Europe, thanks to the cynicism or the opportunism or the phony liberalism of the Politically Correct followers who manipulate or deny the evidence. («Poor little things, look how pitiful they are when they land here with their hopes»). Poor-little-things?!? In Europe the mosques which blossom not under an inflexible respect for every religion but under the shadow of a resurrected bigotry, of a forgotten laicism, literally swarm with terrorists or candidate terrorists. In fact since the New York apocalypse some of them have been arrested. Some weapons of the Merciful-and-Wrathful God have been found. In Italy, for example, many cells of Al Qaeda have been discovered. And now we know that already in 1989 the FBI used to mention a «path of Italian militants», that already in 1989 the mosque of Milan was indicated as a den of terrorists. We know that in the same year a

Milanese-Algerian named Ahmed Ressan had been caught in Seattle with 60 kilos of chemicals for making explosives, that in 1990 two other «Milanese» named Atmani Saif and Fateh Kamel had led the Paris subway's attack, and that from Milan they often moved to Canada. (How strange: two of the nineteen kamikazes of September 11 entered the United States just from Canada...). We also know that Milan and Turin have always been a clearing-house and a recruiting-center for the poor-little-things. Afghans and Bosnians and Kurds included. (A detail, this last one, which juices up the scandal of Ocalan: the Kurdish super-terrorist who was brought to Italy by a Communist congressman and sheltered by the leftist government in an elegant villa near Rome). We also know that the epicenters of the poor-little-things have always been Milan, Turin, Genoa, Rome, Naples, Bologna. That the cities of Cremona, Reggio Emilia, Modena, Florence, Perugia, Trieste, Ravenna, Messina have always had «operative net-works», «logistical bases», «cells-for-the-weapons' traffic». That is, branches of the «Italian Structure for the Homogeneous International Strategy». We also know that like France and England and Germany and Holland and Belgium and Spain, or even more, Italy has always been considered by them «Dar al Harb»: War Territory. Also, a territory where Mos-

lems who refuse to use weapons for the triumph of Islam are considered by the other Moslems «traitors-of-the-faith». And all authorities finally admit that many of the most dangerous terrorists hold passports or identity-cards or residence-permits regularly granted by our over-generous governments. Basically, the same thing that happens in the United States where some of the September 11 kamikazes were admitted by the Immigration Office though they were known to the FBI or CIA. And where, in the name of Civil Rights, you cannot even express your suspicions about someone who has Arab features. Otherwise you are immediately accused of intolerance, prejudice, racism...

We even know where they plot, at this point. And their rendez-vous places are not the mansions or palaces where, risking the gallows, our 1800s' ancestors conspired to free Italy from the subduers. They are the butcher-shops, to begin with. The Islamic butcher-shops that nag every city because the poor-little-things eat only meat of animals which have been slaughtered by throat-cutting then bled and deboned. They also are the Arab grills and the Arab cafés, the Arab brothels and the Arab baths, the Arab shops and of course the mosques. As for the mosques, well: after the New York apocalypse, many Imams have thrown away their mask. And the list is rather long. It in-

cludes the Moroccan butcher whom the Italian jour-
nalists deferentially call Religious Leader of the
Piedmont Islamic Community. I mean the pious
Throat-Cutter who in 1989 came to Turin with a
tourist-visa and who in less than a decade has ope-
ned five butcher-shops plus five mosques, thus
transforming the exquisite city of Cavour into a
filthy kasbah. The virtuous Bleeder who now rai-
ses the portrait of Ousama Bin Laden as a flag and
declares: «As the Koran says, our Holy War is a
right and justified war. All the Brothers of Turin
want to join it». (By the way, dearest Ministers of
the Interiors and Foreign Affairs, why don't you
send him back to Morocco or put him in jail?). It
also contains the President of the Islamic Commu-
nity of Genoa, another glorious city transformed
into a kasbah, as well as the Imams of Naples and
Rome and Bologna. The Imam of Bologna, yes.
The guy who says: «The New York Towers have
been destroyed by the Americans who use Bin La-
den as a shield. If it was not the Americans, it was
the Israelis. In any case Bin Laden is innocent. The
danger is not Bin Laden, it's America». And don't
forget that, twenty-four hours before the New York
apocalypse, in the mosque of Bologna some faith-
ful distributed a leaflet praising terrorism plus
announcing «an exceptional event». Eh! Almost
always grandchildren of the Communists who de-

nied or approved Stalin's massacres, our guests'
protectors maintain that in the Islamic hierarchy
the Imam is an insignificant character: a little cleric
who limits himself to leading the Friday prayer, an
innocuous priest who does not exercise any power.
Bullshit! The Imam is a leading figure who directs
and administers his community with full authority
and power. Pious Throat-Cutter or not, virtuous
Bleeder or not, he is a high priest who manipulates
and influences without any limit the minds and
the actions of his followers. An agit-prop who du-
ring the Friday Prayer flings any sort of political
messages. All the so-called Revolutions of Islam
began through the Imams in the mosques, and the
so-called Iranian Revolution began through the
Imams in the mosques. Not in the Universities,
as the aforesaid grandchildren want us to believe.
Behind every Islamic terrorist there is an Imam,
and Khomeini was an Imam. The major leaders of
Iran were and are Imams, I remind you. And I de-
clare that many Imams (too many) are spiritual
guides of terrorism. Thus, morally speaking, ter-
rorists themselves.

As for the Pearl Harbor which floats over
our heads, there is no doubt that chemical and bio-
logical warfare belongs to the strategy of the SS and
Black Shirts who wave the Koran. During another
one of his video-showings-off, Bin Laden in person

has promised it. And we know that Saddam Hussein has always favored that kind of massacre. We know that he goes on producing bacteria which spread bubonic plague or small pox or leprosy or typhus or anthrax etcetera. Along with that stuff, nuclear weapons plus immense quantities of nerve gas. We know even better that until today that kind of promise has not materialized. In fact our enemies' protectors like to blather that for this too my rage is unfair, exaggerated, deceitful. But the Pearl Harbor I speak of has nothing to do with that kind of promise. It concerns the threat that the FBI spokesmen point out with the words: «It is not a matter of If, it is a matter of When...». A threat I fear more than bubonic plague, more than leprosy, more than nerve gas and even nuclear weapons. A threat that hangs over Europe much more than over America. In fact I speak of the one which imperils our monuments, our art masterpieces, our history's treasures. The essence itself of Western culture.

In saying When-not-If, the FBI spokesmen worry for their own treasures, of course. The Statue of Liberty, the Jefferson Memorial, the Washington Monument, the Liberty Bell, the Golden Gate Bridge, the Brooklyn Bridge, etc. And they are right. I worry for them too. I worry for them as I would worry for the Big Ben or the Westminster

Abbey if I were British. For Notre Dame and the Louvre and the Tour Eiffel if I were French. But I am Italian. Therefore I worry even more for the Sistine Chapel and for the Saint Peter's Dome and for the Coliseum in Rome. For San Marco Square and the museums and the palaces on the Canal Grande in Venice. For the Cathedral and the Atlantic Code and the Last Supper by Leonardo da Vinci in Milan... I am Tuscan, therefore I worry even more for the Pendant Tower and the Miracles Square in Pisa, for the Cathedral and the Town Hall of Siena, for the surviving medieval towers of San Gimignano... I am a Florentine, therefore I worry even more for my Santa Maria del Fiore Cathedral, my Baptistery, my Giotto's Tower, my Pitti Palace, my Uffizi Galleries, my Old Bridge. By the way, the only antique bridge left because all the others were blown up in 1944 by Bin Laden's role model: Adolf Hitler. I also worry for the Laurentian Library with its splendid millenary miniatures, its splendid Vergilian Code. I also worry for the Academy Gallery where we keep Michelangelo's David. (Shamefully naked, my God, therefore particularly blamed by the Koran). And should the poor-little-things destroy one of those treasures, only one, I swear: it is I who would become a holy-warrior. It is I who would become a murderer. So

*listen to me, you followers of a God who preaches
an eye for an eye and a tooth for a tooth. I was born
in the war. I grew up in the war. About war I know
a lot and believe me: I have more balls than your
kamikazes who find the courage to die only when
dying means killing thousands of people. Babies
included. War you wanted, war you want? Good.
As far as I am concerned, war is and war will be.
Until the last breath.*

*   *   *

*Dulcis in fundo. Finally, with a little smile.
And it goes without saying that, like a laugh, sometimes a smile means exactly the opposite. (In my
adolescence I found out that once, while the Fascists were torturing him to know where he had
hidden the weapons parachuted by the Americans
to our Resistance movement, my father laughed.
The revelation froze me and one day I exclaimed:
«Father! Is it true that once, during the tortures,
you laughed?». Father frowned and raucously mur-
mured: «My dear child, in certain cases laughing
is the same as crying. You will see. For sure you will
see...»). Well: when the publication of this book
was announced, Professor Howard Gotlieb of Boston University (the University that for decades*

has been collecting and preserving my work) called me and asked: «How should we define "The Rage and the Pride"?». «I don't know» I answered adding that my small-book was not a novel or a reportage or an essay or a memoir, and in my opinion not even a pamphlet. Then I thought it over. I called him back and said: «Define it a sermon». (The right term, I believe, because in reality what follows is a sermon. It was supposed to be the letter that the editor-in-chief had asked me about the war that the sons of Allah have declared on the West and, while I was writing, it became a sermon). After the publication in Italy Professor Gotlieb called me again and asked: «How did the Italians take it?». «I don't know» I answered adding that a sermon must be judged by the results not by the applauses or the catcalls. Thus, before I could check the results of mine, a lot of time would elapse. A lot. «We cannot expect my rage and my pride to suddenly wake up those who sleep, Professor Gotlieb. As a matter of fact, I don't even know if they will ever wake up».

And I really don't. On the other hand I do know that when my article on September 11 was published, the newspaper sold out more than a million copies. And touching episodes took place. In Rome, for instance, a man bought all the thirty-six copies of a newstand and distributed them to *the passers-by. In Milan a woman did the same with dozens of xeroxes she had made of the text. I also know that thousands of Italians wrote to thank me, that the newspaper's telephone switchboard and internet-lines got jammed for many hours, that only a minority of readers did not agree with me. And what a pity that this did not result from the choice of the letters published under the title «Italy splits over Oriana». In fact I called the editor who had made that choice and yelled at him that if counting is not an opinion, if the votes of those against me hadn't more value than the votes of those with me, it was really unfair to accuse me of dividing my country. Italy does not need any Oriana to split, I added. Italy is splitted at least since the time of the Guelphs and the Ghibellines: from the Middle Ages on, such habit has never changed. Good Lord, even the Garibaldini who came to America to fight in the American Civil War immediately split in two parts. Because only half of them came to New York and enlisted with the Union Army, that is, with the Thirty-Ninth N.Y. Infantry Regiment. The other half chose to enlist with the Confederate Army and went to New Orleans where they formed the Garibaldi Guards of the Sixth Louisiana Militia's Italian Battalion. The battalion that in 1862 became part of the Sixth In-*

fantry Regiment of the European Brigade. They too, raising a tricolor flag with the motto «Vincere o Morire - Victory or Death». They too, distinguishing themselves in the battles of First Bull Run, Cross Keys, North Anna, Bristoe Station, Po River, Mine Run, Spotsylvania, Wilderness, Cold Harbor, Strawberry Plain, Petersburg, up until Appomattox. And do you know what happened on the 2nd of July 1863, in the battle of Gettysburg, when fifty-four thousand North and South soldiers were lost? It happened that the three hundred and sixty-five Garibaldi Guards of the Thirty-Ninth Regiment under the command of General W. S. Hancock found themselves in front of three hundred and sixty Garibaldi Guards of the Sixth Infantry Regiment commanded by General J. Early. The former, in blue uniform. The latter, in grey uniform. Both of them, waving the tricolor flags they had waved together in Italy to make the Unification of Italy. The flags with the motto «Vincere o Morire - Victory or Death». And the former shouting «You-dirty-Southerners», the latter shouting «You-dirty-Northerners», they clashed in a furious hand-to-hand combat for the possession of the mound named Cemetery Hill. Ninety-nine dead among the Garibaldini of the Thirty-Ninth N.Y. Regiment. Sixty, among the Garibaldini of the Eu-

ropean Brigade's Sixth Infantry Regiment. And the next day, in the final charge which took place in the valley, almost twice as much.

I also know that, on the smaller side of the readers who did not agree with me, more than one evil-eye wrote: «Fallaci plays the courageous character because she is very ill and has one foot in the grave». (A wickedness to which I answer no, my dears, no: I do not play the role of the courageous one. I am courageous. I always have been. In peace and in war, vis à vis of the Guelphs and of the Ghibellines. That is, with the so-called Right and the so-called Left. And each time paying a very high price including the price of physical and moral threats, persecutions, slanders. Read me again and you'll see. As for the foot in the grave, to hell with you. I don't swim into an ocean of health, agreed, but the moribunds of my kind always end up with burying the sound people. Don't forget that once I emerged alive from a morgue where I had been thrown as dead). And finally I know that after my article the ugly Italy, the Italy because of which I live in exile, staged a turmoil in favor of the sons of Allah. As a consequence, the ablaze editor-in-chief became a very worried editor-in-chief, blind with worry he took cover behind my detractors and what could have been a good occasion to defend our culture became a squalid fair of squalid

*vanities. A ridiculous chorus of «I-am-here-too,
I-am-here-too». As shadows of a past that never
dies those whom I define «cicadas» lit up a big fire
to burn the Heretic, and up with the howls «To the
stake, to the stake! Allah akbar, Allah akbar!». Up
with the accusations, the condemnations, the insults... Every day an attack or a smear that reminded me the Salem trial. Hang-the-witch, hang-the-
witch. They even mangled and offended my name:
they nicknamed me Orhyena, in their articles... Or
so I was told by those who took the trouble to read
them. I did not. Number one, because I knew what
they would say and did not feel any curiosity.
Number two, because at the end of my article I had
warned that I would not participate in futile di-
scussions or useless polemics. Number three, because the cicadas are invariably persons without
ideas and without qualities: petulant leeches who
invariably place themselves in the shadow of those
who stay in the sun, messengers of paucity. And
their journalism is boring. (My father's elder brother was Bruno Fallaci. A great journalist. He de-
tested journalists, when I worked for the newspapers he only forgave me if I risked my life in some
war. But he was a great journalist. He also was a
great editor-in-chief, and listing the rules of journalism he thundered: «First rule, do not bore the
readers». Cicadas, instead, bore the readers). Num-*

*ber four, because I conduct a very severe and intel-
lectually rich life. I like to study as much as to write, I enjoy staying alone or with learned people,
and this kind of existence does not leave any room
for the messengers of paucity. Finally, because I always follow the advice of an illustrious compatriot
of mine. The overly exiled Dante Alighieri who
said: «Non ti curar di lor ma guarda e passa. Don't
care about them, just look and walk on». As a matter of fact, I go much further than him: while walking on, I don't even look.*

  *However, now I wish to amuse myself
with an exception. I mean with the particular cicada
whose name and sex and identity I ignore and who
has attributed me two serious crimes: not knowing
«A Thousand and One Nights» and not acknow-
ledging that the concept of Zero was defined by
the Arabs. Eh, no, dear Sir or Madam or Half and
Half. No, my petulant leech, my poor messenger of
paucity: I love mathematics, so I'm quite familiar
with the concept of Zero and its origin. Just think
that in my «Inshallah» (by the way a novel built
upon the formula of Boltzmann, the one that says
Entropy-equal-to-the-Constant-of-Boltzmann-
multiplied-by-the-natural-logarithm-of-the-proba-
bilities-of-distribution), just upon the concept of
Zero I fabricated the scene in which the sergeant
kills Passepartout. I did so using a diabolical pro-*

*blem that in 1932 the Normale of Pisa University
set for its students' exams: «Explain why One is
more than Zero». (So diabolical that it can be sol-
ved only «ab absurdo»). Well: in maintaining that
the concept of Zero was defined by the Arabs, you
can only refer to the Arab mathematician Muham-
mad ibn Musa al-Khwārizmī who around 810 A.D.
introduced the decimal numeration with the recurrence of Zero. But you are mistaken. Because Mu-
hammad ibn Musa al-Khwārizmī himself declares
in his writings that the decimal numeration with
the recurrence of Zero is not due to him, no. That he
has taken it from the Indians and particularly from
the renowned Indian mathematician Brahmagupta.
(The author of the astronomy-treatise «Brahma-
Sphuta-Siddhanta», the man who at the very beginning of the Seventh Century focused on the matter). Well... According to some of today's scholars,
Brahmagupta defined the concept of Zero later
than the Mayans. Already in the Fifth Century,
they say, the Mayans used to indicate the birth da-
te of the Universe with the year Zero as well as to
mark the first day of every month with a Zero.
And, when in their calculations a number was missing, they filled the void with a zero. Nevertheless,
in order to mark the zero they did not even use the
strange dot that the Greek would use long after:
they drew a little man with the overturned head.*

This little man with the overturned head is a source of many doubts and misunderstandings, so I inform you that in the history of mathematics nine scholars out of ten give the Zero's paternity to Brahmagupta. And now, dear Sir or Madam or Half and Half, let's talk about «A Thousand and One Nights».

Good Lord, my Lord: whoever told you that I do not know such a gem?!? You see, when I was a little girl I used to sleep in the «library»: improper name that my penniless parents gave to a little room which was literally upholstered with books bought by installments. On the shelf overlooking the minuscule sofa which I called my-bed there was an enormous book with a veiled lady who smiled at me from the jacket, so one night I returned her smile by satisfying my curiosity. That is, by reading the first pages. Mother did not want me to. As soon as she saw the gem in my hands, she confiscated it as if it were a glossary of sins, depravations. «Shame on you, shame on you: this is not for children». But then she thought it over and granted permission. «Okay, read it, read it. It will educate you all the same». Thus, «A Thousand and One Nights» became the fairy-tales of my childhood, and since then it has been part of my books' patrimony. You can find it in my Florence apartment, in my country-house of Tuscany, and also here in

New York where I collect it in several editions. The last one is in French. I bought it from Kenneth Gloss, my antiquity-bookstore of Boston, along with «Les Oeuvres Complètes de Madame De La Fayette» printed by D'Auteil in 1812 and «Les Oeuvres Complètes de Molière» printed by Pierre Didot in 1799. The edition is the one that Hiard, le libraire-éditeur de la Bibliothèque des Amis des Lettres, made in 1832. And I treasure it passionately. But, in all honesty, I don't feel like comparing those adorable fairy-tales with Homer's «Iliad» and «Odyssey». I don't feel like comparing them with Plato's «Dialogues», Vergil's «Aeneid», St. Augustine's «Confessions», Dante Alighieri's «The Divine Comedy», Shakespeare's tragedies and comedies, Kant's «Critique of Pure Reason» and so on. It would not be serious.

End of the little smile and last point to make. A point about which I care a lot because it exposes a problem of dignity, morality, honor.

* * *

I live on my books. On my writings. I live on my royalties: the percentage an author receives on each sold copy. And I am proud of it. I am so even though such percentage is small or I should *say irrelevant. An amount that especially in the case of the paperbacks (the translations, almost worse) does not suffice to purchase half a pencil from a son of Allah who sells pencils along the sidewalks of Florence. (And who has never heard about «A Thousand and One Nights» of course). My royalties, I want them. And I receive them. If I did not, by the way, it would be me the one who goes selling pencils along the sidewalks of Florence. But I do not write for money. I have never written for money. Never. Not even when I was very young and I had an acute need of it to attend the University. (School of Medicine... Which at that time used to cost really a lot). At seventeen I was hired as a reporter by one of the daily newspapers of Florence. And at nineteen I was fired on the spot for refusing to be an ink-slinger. They had ordered me to write an untruthful article on the rally of a famous leader for whom I felt a profound dislike. (The leader of the then Italian Communist Party, Palmiro Togliatti). An article, by the way, that I was not supposed to sign. So I said that I wouldn't write lies, and the managing editor (a fat and pompous Christian-Democrat) bawled back that a journalist is an ink-slinger with the duty to write what he is paid for. «One does not spit on the dish where he eats». Fuming with indignation I replied that he could keep such a dish for himself, that rather than*

*becoming an ink-slinger I would die from starva-
tion, and he fired me on the spot. Which is the reason why, having remained without the salary
I needed to pay the University, I never got the Doc-
torate in Medicine. Yes: nobody has ever been capable of making me write for the bloody money.
What I have written in my life has never had to do
with money. Yes: I have always realized that written words can influence people's minds and actions
more than bombs, than bayonets, and that the responsibility which derives from such awareness
cannot be exercised in exchange for money. As a
consequence, my article on September 11 was not
written for money. The tearing fatigue that destroyed my already worn-out body was not undertaken
for money. My-child, my important novel, did not
go to sleep for the purpose of making me earn more money than I earn with my badly paid royalties.
And here the good stuff comes.*

*It comes because, when the ablaze editor-
in-chief flew to New York and asked me to break
my already broken silence, we did not speak of money. He simply ignored the subject and, as for me,
I simply judged immoral to speak about money in
regard to a work which originated in the death of
so many creatures. In addition, a work which aimed
at unplugging the ears of the deaf and opening the
eyes of the blind etcetera. When the fires were stir-*

red up to burn me on the stake as an heretic, to hang me as a Salem witch, nevertheless, he suddenly informed me that the payment for the tearing fatigue was ready. A «very, very, very lavish payment». So lavish (I don't know the amount and I don't wish to know) that it would have been superfluous to reimburse me the heavy expenses of the long intercontinental calls, he added. Good: though I realized that according to laws of economics paying me was an obligation, (not by chance the articles written for his newspaper by my detractors had been regularly and profusely remunerated), the very-very-very-lavish-payment never reached my pockets. I refused it on the spot. Better: while hearing that the-payment-was-ready, I felt the same embarrassment and amazement I had felt fifty-six years before. That is, when I had discovered that the Italian Army was about to grant me a military discharge for my fighting the nazifascists as a teenage soldier of the Corps Volunteers for Freedom. (The episode I recount in connection with the money I accepted in 1946 to buy the decent shoes that neither I nor my little sisters had).

Well... I'm told that my refusal left the editor-in-chief as petrified as the wife of Lot when she turns to give a last look at Sodoma. I'm also told that many others saw in my gesture an act of naiveté married to haughtiness. (Which may be true).

But both to him and to them the Heretic, the witch, says: now I do have decent shoes, I do. And if I did not, I would prefer to walk barefoot on the snow rather than having in my pockets that very-very-very-lavish-payment. Even one cent of it would have soiled, would soil, my soul.

ORIANA FALLACI

New York, December 2001
Florence, September 2002

You ask me to speak, this time. You ask me to break, this time at least, the silence I chose. The silence that for years I imposed on myself so as not to mix my voice with the voices of the cicadas. And I do it. Because I have heard that in Italy too some rejoice the way the other night the Gaza Palestinians rejoiced on TV: «Victory! Victory!». Men, women, children. (Provided that whoever does such a thing might be defined as a man, a woman, a child). I also heard that some politicians or so-called politicians, as well as various intellectuals or so-called intellectuals who do not have the right to be considered civilized people, substantially behave in the same manner. That they happily say: «Good. Americans got it good». And I am very, very, very angry. Angry with a rage which is cold, lucid, rational. A rage which eliminates any detachment, any indulgence, which orders me to answer them and to spit in their face.

I spit in their face. As angry as I am, last night the Afro-American poetess Maya Angelou roared: «Be angry. It is right to be angry. It is healthy». Well... If it is healthy for me, I don't know. But I do know that it will not be healthy for them. I mean for those who admire the Ousamas Bin Ladens and support them with their comprehension or sympathy or solidarity. Breaking my silence will light up a detonator that for too long has been craving to explode. You'll see.

You also ask me to provide my testimony, to tell you how I lived this Apocalypse, therefore I will start with that. I was at home, my house is in the center of Manhattan, and around 9 in the morning I had the sensation of a danger that maybe did not touch me directly but that for sure concerned me. The sensation you get in combat, when with every pore of your skin you sense the bullet or the rocket arriving, so you prick up your ears and to those who are nearby you shout: «Get down! Down, down!». I rejected it. I said to myself that I was not in Vietnam, for Christsake. I was not in one of the many damn wars that since the Second World War have tormented my life. I was in New York, on a marvelous morning of September. The 11th of September 2001. But the sensation went on possessing me inexplicably, incomprehensibly, so I turned on the TV.

58

Who knows why, the audio did not work. The screen, on the contrary, did. And on each channel (in New York we have about a hundred channels) you could see one of the World Trade Center Towers that from the eightieth floors on was burning like a gigantic match. A short circuit? A scatter-brained pilot who had lost control of his small airplane? Or a well-aimed act of spectacular terrorism? Almost paralyzed I continued to watch and while I was watching, while I was repeating myself those three questions, an airplane appeared on the screen. A big, white, commercial airplane. It was flying very low. Extremely low. And flying low, extremely low, it was directing itself towards the second tower like a bomber that aims at the target, that dives towards the target. Thus, I understood. I also understood because, right in the same moment, the audio came back on and relayed a chorus of choked screams. Choked, incredulous, impotent. «God! Oh, God! God! God! God! Oh, my Go-o-o-o-o-o-d!». Then the airplane slipped into the second tower as a knife slips into a stick of butter.

It was 9:03, now. And don't ask me what I felt in that moment or soon after. I don't know. I don't remember. I was ice-frozen. Even my brain was ice-frozen. I don't even remember if I saw certain things on the first tower or on the second. The people who jumped from the windows of the eightieth and ninetieth and hundredth floors so as not to burn alive, to begin with. Who broke the glass of the windows, climbed over the windows, and jumped the same way we jump from a plane with a parachute. By dozens. And they came down so slowly. Slowly tossing their arms and their hands, slowly swimming in the air... Yes, they seemed to swim in the air. And they never got down. They never arrived. At the thirtieth floors, however, they accelerated. They began to gesticulate in despair, I guess in repentance, as if they were asking for help. Please-help-me-please. And maybe they really did. Then, finally, they dropped like stones and bang! You know it: most of my life I have been in wars... In wars I have seen every kind of horror, by wars I consider myself vaccinated, because of wars nothing surprises me any longer. Not even when I get angry. Not even when I feel disdain. But in wars I have always seen people getting killed. I have never seen people killing themselves, people throwing themselves without parachutes from the windows of an eightieth or a ninetieth or a hundredth floor... They went on jumping and throwing themselves like that until, one around 10 am, one around 10:30, the Towers collapsed and dammit: along with the people who get killed, in wars I have always seen stuff that bursts. Stuff that collapses because it bursts. The two Towers, instead, did not collapse because they burst. The first one collapsed because it imploded, it swallowed itself up. The second one because it melted, liquefied, as if it really was a stick of butter. And everything happened, or so it seemed to me, in a graveyard silence. How possible? Was it really there, that silence, or was it inside me?

Maybe it was inside me. Locked inside that silence, in fact, I heard the news of the third plane fallen on the Pentagon and of the fourth one fallen in a Pennsylvania's wood. Locked inside that silence I began to calculate the number of the dead and I felt strangled by my own breath. Because in the bloodiest combat I followed in Vietnam, a combat near Dak-To, the dead I saw were around four hundred. In the massacre of Mexico City, a massacre where I too was hit by several bullets, around eight hundred. And when assuming I was dead the rescuers abandoned me in a morgue, the corpses I soon found myself amongst seemed to me even more. So, knowing that almost fifty thousand persons usually worked in those Towers, I did not dare to calculate the number. A first evaluation speaks of five or six thousand missing, but there is a difference between the word «missing» and the word «dead». In Vietnam we always distinguished between the missing and the dead. And even if not all the missing were dead... Listen: in my opinion the whole truth will never be known. How could it? Most of the times, only scattered limbs emerge from the debris. A nose here, a finger there. And everywhere you can see a brown mud that seems like ground coffee but in reality is organic matter: the remains of the bodies that in a flash disintegrated, incinerated. Yesterday Mayor Giuliani sent ten thousand body bags, and only a few hundred have been used.

*   *   *

What do I think of the invulnerability that so many in Europe attributed to America, what do I feel for the nineteen kamikazes who wrought this havoc? Listen: for the kamikazes, no respect. No pity. Right: not even pity. I who always end up indulging in pity. Starting with the Japanese kamikazes of the Second World War, I could never stand those who commit suicide in order to kill others. I never considered them valiant and generous people like our Pietro Micca, the Piedmontese soldier who in order to stop the French troops' advance and save the Citadel of Turin on the 29th of August 1706 lit up the gunpowder's deposit and blew up with the enemy. I never considered them soldiers. And even less do I consider them martyrs or heroes, as yelling and spitting his smelly saliva Mr. Arafat defined them to me in 1972. That is, when I interviewed him in Amman: the place where he also trained several Baader-Meinhof's terrorists. I consider them murderers driven by vanity, exhibitionists who instead of pursuing success through movies or politics or sports look for glory in their own death and in the death of others. Who instead of chasing an Oscar award or a Cabinet seat or an Olympic medal, go after a place in the Djanna. The Paradise of the Koran, the Garden of Eden where according to the Prophet all heroes go and make love with the Urì virgins. I bet they are vain even physically. I have under my eyes the photo of the two kamikazes I describe in my book *Inshallah*, the novel which begins with the carnage of 436 American and French soldiers on a peace-mission at Beirut, I keep watching it and... They had that photo taken before going to die, you see, and before having it taken they had gone to the barber. Look at the elaborate haircuts, at the elaborately trimmed mustaches, at the dapper beards, the groomed side-whiskers... But particularly unworthy of respect, of pity, I judge those who performed their death in New York and in

Washington and in Pennsylvania. To begin with, that Muhammed Attah who left two testaments. The one in which he says: «At my funeral I do not want impure beings. Meaning, animals and women». And the one where he adds: «Not even around my grave do I want impure beings. Especially the most impure: pregnant women». Well... It pleases me so much to point out that he will never have any funeral nor grave. Of course nothing, not even a hair, has remained of him either.

My God, guess how hysterical Mr. Arafat would become if he read me. Because we are not on good terms, Mr. Yasser Arafat and I, no. He never forgave me the burning differences of opinion we had during the Amman interview, I never forgave him anything, so I wish him all the worst and he does the same with me. We carefully avoid each other. Should I happen to see him again, however, I would yell in his face what I think about his martyrs and heroes. «First, let me say who the real martyrs are» I would yell. «They are the passengers of the airplanes hijacked and transformed into human bombs by your disciples. Among them, the four-year-old child who disintegrated in the second tower! They are the employees who worked in the Twin Towers and at the Pentagon. They are the four hundred-eighteen firemen and policemen who died to save them. You, big mouth!

And now let me tell you who the real heroes are. They are the passengers on the flight that was supposed to crash into the White House but crashed in the Pennsylvania woods because they rebelled. You moron!». The problem is that now the big mouth, the moron, plays the role of Head of State. He plays the Mussolini ad perpetuum, he visits the Pope, he goes to the White House, he sends condolences to United States President. And in his chameleonic ability to contradict himself, to belie himself, he would be capable of answering that I am right. This liar who has a flash of sincerity only when (in private) he denies Israel's right to exist. This hypocrite who cannot be trusted even when he's asked what time it is. This presumed revolutionary who doesn't even provide his people with a little democracy. I don't say a democracy like Israel's democracy, I say a «little» democracy. This phony warrior who always wears a uniform like Fidel Castro and Pinochet yet delegates the fighting to his poor subjects, to the poor Christs who believe in him. This ignoramus who can't even express a thought, articulate a phrase, put together a rational speech. This eternal terrorist who is only capable of raising terrorists, of keeping his people in the shit, of sending them to die. To kill and to die... But enough with him, enough. He doesn't deserve my time, and

I prefer to talk about the invulnerability that so many, in Europe, attributed to America.

Invulnerability? The more a society is an open and democratic society, the more it is exposed to terrorism. The more a nation is free, the more it risks the massacres which (thanks to the Palestinians) have taken place for so many years in Italy and in the rest of Europe. And which have now reached America. Not by chance the non-democratic countries have always hosted and helped terrorists. The ex-Soviet Union with its satellites and China, to begin with. Then Libya, Iraq, Iran, Syria, Pakistan, Afghanistan, Lebanon. Then Egypt where Anwar Sadat too was killed by terrorists. Then Saudi Arabia where Ousama Bin Laden comes from. Then all the Moslem regions of Africa... In the airports and on the airplanes of those countries I always felt safe, believe me. As serene as a sleeping child. In the European airports and on the European airplanes, instead, I always felt nervous. In the American airports and on the American airplanes, twice as nervous. And in New York, three times so. Why do you think that on Tuesday morning my subconscious felt such an anxiety, such a sensation of danger, and contrarily to my habits I turned on the TV? Why do you think that among the three questions I asked myself while the first tower was burning there was the one of a well-aimed attack of terrorism? Why do you think that I understood the truth as soon as the second airplane appeared? Since America is the richest and strongest country in the world, the most powerful, the most capitalistic, since her military supremacy scares the world, Americans themselves used to cherish the illusion of her invulnerability. But America's vulnerability lies exactly in her strength, my dear. In her richness, her power, her super-capitalism. Meaning, the reasons why she ignites every kind of jealousy and hate.

It also lies in her multiethnic essence, in her tolerance, in the respect for her citizens and her guests. You see, a few millions of Americans are Arab-Moslem. And when a Mustafa or an Alì or a Muhammed comes from Afghanistan to visit his uncle, let's suppose, nobody prevents him from attending a flight school to become a 757 pilot. Or from attending a University to study chemistry and biology: the two sciences one needs to stir up a biological war. He attends them even if the Secret Services fear a hijacking or if they expect that war. But let's go back to the original argument: what are the real features of America, the symbols of her strength and richness and power, super-capitalism, military supremacy? Not jazz and rock and roll, I would say. Not chewing-gum and hamburgers, not Broadway and Hollywood. They are her skyscrapers, her airplanes, her Pentagon, her science, her technology... Those impressive skyscrapers. So tall, so robust, steady, and so beautiful that when you look at them you even forget the Pyramids and the divine palaces of our past. Those ubiquitous airplanes and helicopters. So huge, so quick, so capable of transporting any transportable matter. Prefabricated houses, fresh flowers, fresh fish, rescued elephants, penniless tourists, combat troops, armored tanks, atomic bombs... (Besides, it is America who developed air war to the point of hysteria: remember?). That terrifying Pentagon. That sombre fortress which would scare Napoleon and Gengis Khan together. That omnipresent omnipotent omnivorous science. That overwhelming technology which has changed our daily existence, our centenarian way of life, in a flash. And where did Ousama Bin Laden hit? On the skyscrapers, on the Pentagon. How? With her science, her technology. By the way: do you know what impresses me mostly about this grim ultra-millionaire, this ex-playboy who at twenty used to frolic in night clubs and now assignes himself the Ferocious Saladin's duties? The fact that his boundless patrimony derives from the earnings of a corporation which is specialized in demolition, and that in this field he is a real expert. A master, an unsurpassable champion.

Could I interview him, in fact, one of my questions would be just on this matter. I mean, on the pleasure that almost certainly his psyche gets from destruction. And needless to say that another question would be on his defunct ultra-polygamist father who begot fifty-four children and used to portray the seventeenth one (him) with these words: «He is the nicest, the sweetest, the best». Another would be on his sisters who when in London or on the Riviera like to be photographed with uncovered heads, uncovered faces. Their plump breasts well exposed by tight-fitting sweaters, their fat buttocks well displayed by tight-fitting pants. No burkah, no chador. Still another, on the relationship that he continues to maintain with Saudi Arabia. That stinky bank-vault. That medieval feud which enslaves us with its fucking oil, its greed, its backwardness, its secret feeding any terrorism. I would ask him: «Mister Bin Laden, Sir, how much money does Al Qaeda receive from your compatriots and from the members of the Royal Family?». But, rather than wasting my time with questions, maybe I should simply inform him that he has not brought New York to its knees. And to inform him that he has not, I should tell him what Bobby, an eight-year-old boy of Manhattan, taught us yesterday morning.

«My Mom always used to say: "Bobby, if you get lost on the way home, have no fear. Look at the two Towers and remember that we live ten blocks away on the Hudson River". Now the Towers are gone. Evil people wiped them out with those who were inside, and for many days I kept asking myself: "Bobby, how will you go home if you get lost now?" But then I concluded: "Bobby, in this world there are good people also. If you get lost now, some good person will help you instead of the Towers. The important thing is to have no fear"».

And on this matter I must add a few things which have to do with us.

* * *

When you came here, last week, I saw you amazed by the heroic efficiency and by the admirable unity with which Americans have faced this apocalypse. Oh, yes: in spite of all the defects we continuously point out and condemn (but those of us Europeans are much worse, as we'll see), America is a country that has a lot to teach us. And apropos of her heroic efficiency let me sing a paean for the Mayor of New York. That Rudolph Giuliani whom the Italians should thank on their knees because (like many firemen and policemen dead in the Towers) he has an Italian last name, he is of Italian descent, he makes us cut a fine figure in front of the whole world... Listen to me, that is to say to a person who never praises anybody beginning with herself: what a great Mayor that Rudolph Giuliani is! A Mayor worthy of another great Mayor with the Italian last name, Fiorello La Guardia, and many of our Mayors should learn from him. Their heads covered with ashes, they should go to his townhall and bow and ask: «Mister Giuliani, Sir, could you please teach us how to make our job?». He does not delegate his duties to others, as they do. He does not divide himself between the task of Mayor and the one of Congressman, as they do. When the apocalypse occurred, he immediately ran to the Towers and risked getting incinerated with the others. He saved himself by an inch and, in less than three days, he put a city of nine million inhabitants back on its feet. Almost two million, in Manhattan. How he did it, it's a mistery. (He has my same problem, you know. Years ago the damn cancer got him too). But he never tires. You never see in him a sign of idleness, of weariness, of fear. «The first of the Human Rights is Freedom from Fear. Do not have fear» he says. The fact is that he says it and behaves this way because around him there are people who resemble him. People with balls. For instance, the fireman

71

whom yesterday I saw on TV. A guy with hair as blond as ripe corn, eyes as blue as clean sea, and another Italian name: Jimmy Grillo. They asked him whether he would change his job. He answered: «I am a fireman and I shall be a fireman all my life. Always here, always in New York. To protect my city and my family and my friends».

As for their admirable capacity to unite, the almost martial compactness with which the Americans react to misfortunes and to enemies, look: I must admit that on September 11 I was amazed too. Of course, I did know that such compactness had well revealed itself in the past. Just to give an example, at the time of Pearl Harbor: when the country united around Roosevelt and Roosevelt declared war upon Hitler's Germany and Mussolini's Italy and Hirohito's Japan. Or, in the same spirit, after John Kennedy's assassination. But Kennedy's assassination had been followed by the lacerating division caused by the war in Vietnam, and in a certain sense that division had reminded me of their Civil War. Thus, when I saw blacks and whites hugging each other, Democrats and Republicans singing together «God Bless America», I reacted just like you. The same, when I heard Bill Clinton (a person for whom I never felt any tenderness) declare: «Let us bind together around Bush, let us trust our President». The same, when those words were repeated by his Senator wife. By Hillary Rodham. The same, when they were reiterated by Senator Joe Lieberman. (Only the defeated Al Gore has maintained, and still does, a painfully squalid silence). The same, when the Congress voted unanimously to accept the war. The same, when I discovered that their motto is the noble Latin aphorism that reads: «Ex Pluribus Unum. From many, one». (That is, All for One). Yes, I got amazed and now I feel jealous. Jealous and touched. Oh, if our country could learn their lesson! It is such a divided country, our country. So sectarian, so poisoned by its old tribal miseries! They are unable to stay together even within their own political parties, the Italians. Even within the same ideology they only care for their own petty success, their own petty glory. They betray each other, they accuse each other, they throw shit on each other... I am absolutely sure that, if Ousama Bin Laden would destroy the Tower of Giotto or the Tower of Pisa, the Italian opposition would blame the government and the Italian government would blame the opposition; the bosses of the government and the bosses of the opposition would blame their own comrades. And now let me explain you where the extraordinary capability that

73

Americans have of uniting, of responding with almost martial compactness to misfortunes and enemies, comes from.

It comes from their patriotism. I don't know if you have seen on TV what happened when Bush came here to thank the rescue-workers who dig in that sort of ground coffee without giving up, so if you ask them how they do it they answer: «I can allow myself to be exhausted not to be defeated». I don't know if you have seen them waving the American flags and chanting «U-s-a, U-s-a, U-s-a». Well, I have. And in a totalitarian country I would have thought: «Look how well the Power organized it!». In America, no. In America you cannot organize such things. You cannot arrange them, you cannot impose them. Especially in a metropolis as disenchanted as New York and with laborers like the laborers of New York. They are hardnosed guys, the laborers of New York. Tough-tempered, freer than the wind. Individuals, I tell you, who don't even obey their trade-unions. But if you touch their Patria... In English the word «Patria» does not exist. To say «patria» you must couple two words and say Fatherland or Motherland or Nativeland or simply My Country. Yet the substantive «patriotism» exists, the adjective «patriotic» exists. And apart from France, maybe, I cannot imagine another country more patriotic than America. Oh, I felt a sort of humiliation in watching those laborers who spontaneously waved their flags and roared «U-s-a, U-s-a, U-s-a». I did because I never saw the Italian laborers waving the tricolor** and roaring Italy-Italy-Italy. Never. I saw them waving so many red flags. Rivers, lakes, oceans, of red flags. But the Italian flag, never. Badly guided or tyrannized by a Communist Party that served the Soviet Union, they always left the tricolor to their adversaries. And nobody can say that their adversaries made good use of it. As a result, today the tricolor can be seen only at the Olympic Games when by chance we win a medal, or in the stadiums when we play an international soccer-game. The only occasion when you hear the proud shouting «Italy-Italy-Italy».

Yes, there is a big difference between a nation where the Fatherland-Motherland flag is waved only by the ruffians of the stadiums or by

** *Author's note.* The tricolor is a flag composed by three bands of different colors. Italians call their flag (which has a green and a white and a red vertical band) simply Tricolor. A habit in use since the Risorgimento. That is, since the struggles for the Unification of Italy, when the green and white and red tricolor (but for unspecified reasons we say white red and green, that is, bianco rosso e verde) was created on the model of the red and white and blue tricolor born in France out of the French Revolution.

the winners of an Olympic medal, and a nation where it is waved by all its citizens. For instance, by the patriotic laborers who dig in that sort of ground coffee to rescue a few limbs of the creatures disintegrated by the sons of Allah and find nothing but a nose here and a finger there.

* * *

The fact is that America is a very special country, my dear. A country to really envy, yes, a country to really be jealous of. And for reasons which have nothing to do with her richness, her immense power, her military supremacy. Do you know why? Because America is a nation that arose from a need of the soul, the need for a Patria, and from the most sublime idea ever conceived in the West: the idea of Liberty married to the idea of Equality. It is a special country also because this happened when the idea of Liberty was not in fashion. The idea of Equality, even less. Only certain philosophers called Illuminists or Enlighteners spoke about these things, at that time. Only an enormous and expensive book in seventeen volumes (which with the eighteen Tables-volumes would become thirty-five) published in France under the direction of a certain Diderot and of a certain

D'Alembert, (the one called *Encyclopédie*, Universal Dictionary of Art and Science), explained those concepts. And apart from the intellectuals, apart from the aristocrats who had the money to buy the seventeen then thirty-five volumes of the Big Expensive Book or the books which had inspired it, who knew about Illuminism or Enlightenment at that time? Who fought for the sublime idea? Not even the revolutionaries of the French Revolution, given the fact that the French Revolution started in 1789. Meaning, fifteen years after the American Revolution which started in 1776 but had blossomed in 1774. (A detail that the anti-American leftists always seem to forget or pretend to forget). But, above all, America is a special country because the idea of Liberty married to the idea of Equality was understood by peasants who were mostly illiterate or anyway uneducated. The peasants of the thirteen American colonies. And because it materialized thanks to extraordinary leaders, men of great culture and great quality and great imagination: the Founding Fathers. For Christsake, does anybody remember the names Benjamin Franklin, Thomas Jefferson, Thomas Paine, John Adams, George Washington, etcetera, etcetera, amen? Nothing in common with the pettifogging lawyers, that is, the «avvocaticchi» (as Vittorio Alfieri contemptuously used to call them) of the French Revolution. Nothing to do with the gloomy and perfidious executioners of its Terror: the various Marat, Danton, Desmoulins, Saint-Just, Robespierre and so on. They were men, the Founding Fathers, who knew Greek and Latin as our teachers of Greek and Latin never will. Men who used to read Archimedes and Aristotle and Plato in Greek, Seneca and Cicero and Vergil in Latin. Men who studied the principles of Greek democracy as not even the Marxists of my time used to study the Theory of Plusvalue. (Provided that the Marxists of my time really did). Jefferson even knew Italian. (He called it Tuscan). In Italian he spoke and wrote and read with considerable ease. In fact, along with the two thousand vine cuttings and the one thousand olive bedders and the music sheets that in Virginia could not be easily found, in 1774 the Florentine doctor Filippo Mazzei brought him five copies of a certain book written by a certain Cesare Beccaria: *Dei Delitti e delle Pene* («On Crimes and Punishments»). As for the self-taught Benjamin Franklin, he was a genius. A scientist, a typographer, a writer, an editor, a journalist, a politician, an inventor. He discovered the electrical nature of lightning, for instance. He invented the lightning-rod, and the piped stove to warm up the rooms without a fireplace. (In fact the Granduke of Tuscany, Pietro Leopoldo, bought two of them for his studio at Pitti Palace in Florence). And it was with these extraordinary leaders, these men of great culture and great quality and great imagination, that in 1776 the mostly illiterate or uneducated peasants of the thirteen American colonies rebelled against England and fought the War for Independence. The American Revolution.

They fought it, in spite of the blood that every war costs, without the French Revolution's abominations. Without the guillotine's horror, without Toulon's and Lyon's and Bordeaux's massacres, without Vandée's carnages. They fought it thanks to a piece of paper which along with the need of the soul, the need for a Patria, concretized the sublime idea of Liberty married to Equality: the Declaration of Independence. «We hold these truths to be self-evident... That all men are created equal, that they are endowed by their Creator with certain inalienable rights... That among these are Life, Liberty and the Pursuit of Happiness... That to secure these rights, governments are instituted among men...». And this paper that from the French Revolution on the whole West has copied, from which each of us has drawn inspiration, still constitutes the backbone of America. Her vital lymph. Know why? Because it transforms the subjects into citizens. Because it turns the plebes into people. Because it invites, no, it orders the plebes turned into citizens to rebel against tyranny and to govern themselves. To express their individualities, to search for their own happiness. (Something that for the poor, for the plebes, means to get rich). The exact contrary, in short, of what the Communists used to do with their practice of forbidding people to govern themselves, to express themselves, to get rich. With their practice of installing His Majesty the State on the throne. «Communism is a monarchic regime, an old style monarchy» my intelligent father used to say. «As such, it cuts off the balls of men. And when a man gets his balls cut off, he is no longer a man». He also used to say that instead of rescuing the plebes, Communism turns everybody into plebes. It makes everybody die of poverty and starvation, it prevents the plebes from being rescued.

Well: in my opinion America rescues, redeemes, the plebes. Basically, they are all plebeian, in America. White and black, yellow and brown, stupid and intelligent, poor and rich. As a matter of fact, in many cases the most plebeian are just the rich. Such boors! You realize at once that they never read «Monsignor della Casa's Good Manners», that they never had any familiarity with sophistication and refinement. The food they usually eat, for instance. The way they usually dress. Most of them are so inelegant that, in comparison, the Queen of England looks as chic as a high-class model.

But they are rescued, by God! They are redeemed! And in this world there is nothing more vital, more powerful, more inexorable, than Redeemed Plebes, than Rescued Plebes. You always break your nose with the Rescued Plebes, the Redeemed Plebes. And, in one way or another, all have broken their noses with America. The English, the Germans, the Russians, the Mexicans, the Nazis, the Fascists, the Communists... In the end, even Ho Chi Minh's Vietnamese. After the victory, in fact, they too had to come to terms with hated America. And when ex-president Clinton went to pay them a little visit, they touched the sky with their fingers. «Bienvenu, Your Excellence, bienvenu! Shall we faire businèss avec America, ouì? Beaucoup money, much argent, ouì?». The problem is that the sons of Allah are not Vietnamese. And with them the war will be very tough. Very long, very difficult, very tough. Unless we Europeans stop shitting in our pants and playing the double-game with the enemy, giving up our dignity. An opinion I respectfully offer to the Pope too.

(Tell me, Holy Father: is it true that some time ago you asked the sons of Allah to forgive the Crusades that Your predecessors fought to take back the Holy Sepulchre? But did the sons of Allah ever ask you to be forgiven for having taken the Holy Sepulchre? Did they ever apologize for having subjugated over seven centuries the super-Catholic Iberian peninsula, the whole Portugal and three quarters of Spain, so that if Isabella of Castile and Ferdinando of Aragon had not chased them out in 1490 we all would speak Arabic? The question intrigues me, Holy Father, because they never asked me any forgiveness for the crimes that in the seventeenth and eighteenth century the Saracens committed along the coasts of Tuscany and in the Mediterranean. I mean when they kidnapped my ancestors, they chained up their legs and their arms and their necks, they took them to Algiers or Tunis or Tangier or Constantinople and sold them in the bazaars. They kept them slaves for the rest of their lives, the young women inside the harems, they punished their attempts to escape by cutting their throats: remember? Of course, you remember. The Society for the Liberation of the White Slaves held by them in Algeria, in Tunisia, in Morocco, in Turkey etcetera was founded by Italian friars: right? And it was the Catholic Church that negotiated the release of those who had the money to pay their ransom: right? You really bewilder me, Most Holy Father. Because you have worked so hard to see the Soviet Union collapse. My generation, a generation which has lived its entire existence in the fear of the Third World War, must thank especially you for the miracle in which none of us believed: a Europe free from the nightmare of Communism, a Russia which asks to enter into Nato, a Leningrad which is named again Saint Petersburg, a Putin who is Bush's best friend. His best ally. And after such victory you wink at individuals who are worse than Stalin, you flirt with the same ones who still would like to build mosques inside the Vatican? Most Holy Father... In all respect, you remind me of the German-Jewish bankers who in the 1930s, hoping to save themselves, lent money to Hitler. And who a few years later ended in his crematory ovens).

*   *   *

I don't speak, of course, to the vultures who seeing the September 11's images scornfully giggle «Good. Americans-got-it-good». I speak to the people who, though neither stupid nor evil, delude themselves in pietism or uncertainty or doubt. And to them I say: Wake up, folks, wake up! As intimidated as you are by the fear of going against the stream and looking racist (a grossly erroneous word, by the way, because the problem has nothing to do with a race: it has to do with a religion) you don't understand or don't want to understand that a Reverse Crusade is on march. As blinded as you are by the myopia and the stupidity of the Politically Correct, you don't realize or don't want to realize that a war of religion is being carried out. A war they call Jihad. A war that does not aim at the conquest of our territory maybe, (maybe?), but certainly aims at the conquest of our souls and at the disappearance of our freedom. A war which is conducted to destroy our civilization, our way of living and dying, of praying or not praying, of eating and drinking and dressing and studying and enjoying Life. As numbed as you are by the propaganda of the falsehood, you don't put or do not want to put in your mind that if we do not defend ourselves, if we do not fight, the Jihad will win. It will win, yes, and destroy the world that somehow or other we have been able to build. To change, to improve, to make more intelligent, less bigoted or not bigoted at all. It will cancel our culture, our art, our science, our identity, our morals, our values, our pleasures... By God! Don't you see that all these Ousamas Bin Ladens consider themselves authorized to kill you and your children because you drink alcohol, because you don't grow the long beard and refuse the chador or the burkah, because you go to the theater and to the movies, because you love music and sing a song, because you dance and watch television, because you wear the miniskirt or the shorts, because on the beach and by the swimming pool you sunbathe almost naked or naked, because you make love when you want and with whom you want, or because you don't believe in God?!? I am an atheist, thank God. And I have no intention of being punished for this by retrograde bigots who, instead of contributing to the improvement of humanity, salaam and squawk prayers five times a day.

For twenty years I have been repeating it. Twenty. With a certain mildness, not with this rage and this pride, twenty years ago I wrote an editorial. It was the editorial of a person inured to living with all races and habits and beliefs, of a woman accustomed to opposing any fascism and any intolerance, of a laic without any taboos. But it was also the scream of a Westerner full of indignation towards the idiots who did not smell the bad smell of a Holy War to come, and who tolerated the abuses that the sons of Allah were committing in Europe with their terrorism... My reasoning went more or less this way, twenty years ago: «What logic is there in respecting those who do not respect us? What dignity is there in defending their culture or supposed culture when they show contempt for ours? I want to defend my culture, not theirs, and I inform you that I like Dante Alighieri and Shakespeare and Goethe and Verlaine and Walt Whitman and Leopardi much more than Omar Khāyyām». Well:

I got crucified. «You racist, dirty racist!». It was our cicadas who crucified me with the fraudolent word «racist». And later, that is during the Soviet invasion of Afghanistan, they did it again. They did it because, each time the bearded warriors yelled Allah-akbar while shooting the mortar, I had a foreboding and said: «Let's admit it. Soviets are what they are, but in this case we should thank them». Besides, I got crucified also when I pointed out what they used to do to the Soviet prisoners. I mean when they cut off their arms and their legs. (The same atrocity, don't forget, they performed at the end of the nineteenth century on Queen Victoria's ambassadors and on other European diplomats based in Kabul. After such mutilation they decapitated the victim still alive, and with the cut head they played buskachi. A sort of Afghan polo. As for the arms and the legs, they sold them as trophies in the bazaar...). I got crucified then too, yes. They didn't even like the fact that I cried on the armless and legless Ukrainian recruits who, having been abandoned by those barbarians and recovered by their comrades, now lay in the field-hospitals imploring let-me-die. They called me «racist» for that too, remember? While calling me racist they cheered the Americans who crazy with fear of the Soviet Union gave the barbarians support and weapons, trained a young Saudi named Ousama Bin Laden and shouted: «Hooray the heroic Afghan people! Down with the Soviets! Soviets get out of Afghanistaaan!». Well: the Soviets got out. Ousama Bin Laden remained, and sent his kamikazes to America. Happy now?

Some are neither happy nor unhappy. They simply don't care. Why should we, they object, America is far away. There is an Ocean between America and Europe. Eh, no, my dears. There is not an Ocean: there is a thread of water. Because when the destiny of the West is in question, when the survival of our civilization is in jeopardy, New York is us. America is us. We Italians, we French, we English, we Germans, we Swiss, Austrians, Dutch, Hungarians, Slovenians, Poles, Belgians, Spanish, Greeks, Portuguese, Scandinavians, Russians... Yes: also Russians, given the fact that Moscow shares our problem with the terrorism carried out by the Moslems of Chechnya. America is us, I tell you. So, if America collapses, Europe collapses. The whole of the West collapses. We all collapse. And not only financially, that is, in the sole way many fear. (Once, I was young and naïve, I said to playwright Arthur Miller: «You Americans measure everything with money, you only worry about the bloody money». And Arthur Miller laughed, snapped back: «Don't you?»). We collapse in every way, my dears. Because our civilization dies out and we end up with the minarets in place of the bell-towers, with the burkah in place of the mini-skirt, with the camel-milk in place of our little-drink... Can't you understand it, dammit? Blair did. Soon after the tragedy he came here and renewed his solidarity to Bush. Not a solidarity based on chatters and moans: a solidarity based on facts. That is, on military alliance. Chirac did not. As you know, he too came here. On a visit arranged a long time before, not an ad hoc one. He came, he saw the ruins of the Twin Towers, he realized that the dead were an unutterable number, but he did not compromise himself. During the CNN interview, four times he was asked by Christiane Amanpour in what way and to what extent the French intended to align against the Jihad. And four times he avoided the answer, he slithered away like an eel. In such a devious and fearful manner, I mean, that I felt like yelling: «Monsieur le President, don't you remember the landing in Normandy? Don't you know how many Americans died in Normandy to chase the Nazis from France?!?».

The trouble is that I don't see any Richard Lion-heart among the other European leaders either. And even less do I see them in my country where, to the day of this letter, end of September 2001, no accomplice or suspected accomplice of

Ousama Bin Laden has been identified and arrested as yet. Come on, Mister Prime Minister of Italy: the mosques of Milan and Turin and Rome simply overflow with terrorists or candidate terrorists who dream of blowing up our bell-towers, our domes: are your policemen so incapable? Are your Secret Service men so disinformed, so shy? Are your officials so inept? And are all our bearded guests so innocent, so unrelated to what happened in America? Or is it your fear that prevents you from identifying and arresting the above-mentioned guys? Good Lord, I don't deny anybody the right to have fear. A thousand times I have written that whoever claims not to know fear is either a liar or an idiot or both. But in Life and in History there are moments when fear is not permitted. Moments when fear is immoral and uncivilized. And those who out of weakness or stupidity (or the habit of keeping one foot in two shoes) avoid the obligations imposed by this war, are not only cowards: they are masochists.

* * *

Masochists, yes, masochists. And on this subject let's finally speak of what you call Contrast-Between-the-Two-Cultures. The two?!? If you really want to know, I feel uncomfortable even when you pronounce the words «two cultures». That is, when you put them on the same level as if they were two parallel entities. Two realities of equal weight and value. Don't be so humble, my dear. Because behind our culture there is Homer, there is Pheidias, there is Socrates, there is Plato, there is Aristotle, there is Archimedes. There is Ancient Greece with its divine sculpture and architecture and poetry and philosophy, with its principle of democracy. There is Ancient Rome with all its grandeur, its universality, its concept of the Law, its literature, its palaces, its amphitheaters, its aqueducts, its bridges, its streets built all over the then known world... There is a revolutionary called Jesus who died on the cross to teach us the concept of love and justice. (And so much the worse for us if we didn't learn it). There is also a Church that gave us the Inquisition, I know. A Church that through the Inquisition tormented and tortured us, burned us a thousand times on the stake. A Church that oppressed us for centuries, that for centuries obliged us to only paint and sculpt Christs and Madonnas and Martyrs and Saints. A Church that almost killed Galileo Galilei, humiliated him, compelled him to betray himself and his knowledge... But this Church also gave a tremendous contribution to the History of Thought, and after the Inquisition began to change. Not even an anti-clerical like me can deny it. Then there is the cultural awakening that started and flourished in Florence, in Tuscany, to replace Man at the center of the Universe and concile his need of freedom with his need of God. I mean the Renaissance. And thanks to the Renaissance there is Leonardo da Vinci, Michelangelo, Donatello, Raffaello, Lorenzo il Magnifico. (I choose the first names that come to my mind). There is also the heritage left by Erasmus from Rotterdam and Montaigne and Thomas More and Cartesius. There is also the Enlightenment, I mean Rousseau and Voltaire and the *Encyclopédie*. There is also the music of Mozart and Bach and Beethoven and Rossini and Donizetti up to Verdi and Puccini and company. (That music without which we cannot live and which in the Moslem culture or presumed culture is a shame, a great crime: woe betide those who whistle a song or hum a lullaby. «At most I can concede you a march for the soldiers» Khomeini said to me during the Qom interview). Finally there is our Science, by God. And the technology that derives from it. A science which in a few centuries has made breathtaking discoveries, has really changed the face of this planet. A technology which has produced and produces miracles worthy of Merlin the Wizard... Enough with bullshit, my dear: Coperni-

cus, Galileo, Newton, Darwin, Pasteur, Einstein
were not followers of the Prophet. Were they? The
motor, the telegraph, the light-bulb, I mean the use
of electricity, the photograph, the telephone, the
radio, the television, have not been invented by some mullahs or some ayatollahs. Have they? The
train, the automobile, the airplane, the helicopter,
(that Leonardo da Vinci fancied and designed),
the spacecrafts with which we have gone to the
Moon and to Mars and will soon go God knows
where, the same. Right? The heart and liver and
eyes and lungs' transplant, the cures for cancer,
the genome's disclosure, as well. Wrong? And let
us not forget the standard of life that Western culture has achieved at every level of society. In the
West we don't any longer die of starvation and cu-
rable diseases as they do in the Moslem countries.
Right or wrong? But even if all these were unim-
portant achievements, (which I doubt), tell me:
what are the conquests of the other culture, the
culture of the bigots with the beard and the chador and the burkah?

Look and search, search and look, I can
only find the Prophet with his sacred book that
sounds preposterous even when it plagiarizes the
Bible and the Gospels and the Torah and the Hel-
lenistic thinkers. I only find Averroè with his indisputable merits of scholar, (Aristotle's *Commen-*

taries and so on), Omar Khāyyām with his fine
poetry, plus a few beautiful mosques. No other
achievement in the field of art and in the garden of
Thought. No accomplishment in the domain of
science, of technology, of welfare... When I mention this truth, some object with the word mathematics. Again yelling, again spitting in my face his
smelly saliva, in 1972 Arafat said to me that his
culture was «superior» to mine because his ancestors had invented mathematics and numbers. (By
the way, cicadas: how come he can use the word
«superior» and I cannot?). But, along with a weak
intelligence and strong ignorance, Arafat has a very
short memory. No, Mr. Big Mouth, let's clear it up
once and for all: your ancestors did not invent mathematics. Mathematics was invented more or less
simultaneously by the Arabs, the Indians, the
Greeks, the Mayans, the Mesopotamians. Go and
check. Nor did your ancestors invent numbers.
They simply invented a new way of writing them.
The way that we Unfaithful have adopted, thus
facilitating and speeding the discoveries you never made. That invention is highly commendable,
I agree. Undoubtedly meritorious. But it is also in-
sufficient to define Islamic culture superior to
Western culture. As a consequence, I feel fully authorized to affirm that, apart from Averroè and some poets and some mosques and the way of wri-

ting the numbers, your ancestors have substantially left a book and that's all. I mean that Koran which for a thousand and four hundred years has tormented humanity even more than the Bible or the Gospels and the Torah together. And now let me see why the cicadas, especially the European ones, respect it more than they used to respect Karl Marx's *Das Kapital*.

Because of its mendacious, hypocritical, phony preaching Peace and Fraternity and Justice, maybe? Oh! To keep his Arab-Americans quiet, loyal, even George W. Bush keeps on saying that Islam preaches peace and fraternity and justice. But in the name of logic: if this Koran is so peaceful and fraternal and just, how do we explain its «an-eye-for-an-eye-and-a-tooth-for-a-tooth» that we find also in the Bible and the Torah, true, but that for them is the Salt of Life? How do we explain the imposition of the chador and the burkah, that burkah under which Moslem women become shapeless bundles and look at the world through a minuscule web? How do we explain the fact that in most of Islam they cannot go to school, cannot go to the doctor, have no right whatsoever, count less than a camel, etcetera etcetera amen? How do we explain the monstrosity of lapidation or decapitation for the adulterous wives? (Not for the adulterous husbands). How do we justify the death penalty on drinkers of alcohol and the mutilation penalty on thieves, for the first theft the left hand, for the second the right hand, for the third the left foot, then I don't know what? This too is stated in the Koran: yes or no? And it does not seem to me very fair. It does not seem to me very fraternal. It does not seem to me very peaceful. It does not seem to me very intelligent either... And speaking of intelligence: why don't the Italian ultra-leftists cicadas accept these remarks? Why in reading or hearing them do they go crazy and shout «Unbearable, intolerable, scandalous»? Have they all converted to Islam or do they behave this way in order to please their new partner, I mean, the inexplicably pro-Islam Catholic Church? Well... My uncle Bruno was right when he said: «Italy, which did not have the Reformation, is the country that lives more intensely and disastrously the Counter-Reformation».

Here is, then, my answer to your question on what you call Contrast-Between-the-Two-Cultures. In this world there is room for everybody. In their own houses, their own countries, people do what they want. Therefore, if in the Moslem countries women are so stupid as to wear the chador or the burkah, if they are so silly as to accept the fact of counting less than a camel, if they are so foolish as to marry a dissolute who wants four wives, all the worse for them. If their men are so silly as to refuse a glass of wine or beer, the same. I will not be the one who interferes with their choices. I was educated in the concept of freedom, dammit, and my mother used to say: «The world is interesting because it's various». But if they try to impose those insanities on me, on my life, my country, if they want to substitute my culture with their culture or presumed culture... They do. Ousama Bin Laden has declared that the whole planet Earth must become Moslem, that with good or bad manners he will convert us, that to achieve this purpose he kills us, he will continue to kill us. And this cannot be accepted even by the ultra simpleton or cynical supporter of Islam. So imagine if it can be accepted by me. As a matter of fact, it gives me a tremendous urgency to turn the tables and kill him... The problem is that the solution does not depend upon the death of Ousama Bin Laden. Because the Ousamas Bin Ladens are too many, by now: as cloned as the sheep of our research-laboratories. Moreover, they are no longer the bold Moors who conquered Spain and Portugal riding camels and fighting with golden scimitars.

Times change. Today they are the shrewd tricksters to whom we teach how to pilot a 757 jet, how to use a sophisticated computer, how to fabricate a nuclear weapon. How to destroy or block up an electrical system, a communication system, a financial system, how to unleash an epidemic virus. How to blackmail a government, how to manipulate a Pope, how to seduce and exploit the media and the intellectual or so-called intellectual world. That is, how to influence Western minds (including the minds of the people in good faith) by controlling their daily environment. In fact the best trained and the more intelligent do not stay in the Moslem countries, in the caves of Afghanistan or in the mosques of Iran and Pakistan. They stay in our countries, in our cities, our universities, our business companies. They have excellent bonds with our churches, our banks, our televisions, our radios, our newspapers, our publishers, our academic organizations, our unions, our political parties. They nest in the ganglia of our technology. Worse: they live in the heart of a society that hosts them without questioning their differences, without checking their bad intentions, without penalizing their sullen fanaticism. A society that keeps them in the spirit of its permissive democracy, its unconstrained broadmindedness, its Christian pity, its liberal principles, its civilized laws. The laws that have abolished torture and capital punishment, that do not allow to arrest you if a crime has not been committed, do not authorize to judge you if you are not defended by a lawyer, do not permit to condemn you if the accusation has not been proved. The laws or should I say the loopholes that consent to cancel a sentence or to release a delinquent. As for those loopholes, well... Isn't it thanks to them that our guests settle in our territory and they intrude in our life and vex and boss us? During a synod that the Vatican held on October 1999 to discuss the rapports between Christians and Moslems, an eminent Islam scholar addressed the stunned audience declaring with placid effrontery: «By means of your democracy we shall invade you, by means of our religion we shall dominate you». (The worrying report is provided by one of the participants: His Eminence monsignor Giuseppe Bernardini, archbishop in the Turkish Diocese of Smyrns).

As you see, their Reverse Crusade does not need a modern Ferocious Saladin or some kind of Napoleon to take place and develop. With or without Saladins and Napoleons, it is an irreversible fact. An ever-growing reality that the West senselessly feeds and backs up. Which is the reason why those Crusaders become more and more, demand more and more, boss around more and more. Also, the reason why (if we continue to stay inert) they will become always more and more. They will demand always more and more, they

98

will vex and boss us always more and more. Till the point of subduing us. Therefore, dealing with them is impossible. Attempting a dialogue, unthinkable. Showing indulgence, suicidal. And he or she who believes the contrary is a fool.

*   *   *

Take it from someone who has known that vast world rather well. In Iran, in Pakistan, in Bangladesh, in Saudi Arabia, in Kuwait, in Libya, in Jordan, in Lebanon, in Syria, in Africa, and even in Italy. Someone who has known it, yes, and who also through grotesque events has received chilly confirmations of what she maintains. Good Heavens, I shall never forget what happened in Rome when I asked for an Iranian visa (Khomeini interview) and I went to the Iranian Embassy with my nails painted red. In the eyes of a very fanatic Moslem, a sign of immorality. A fellony for which the culprit can have all her fingers amputated. Shaking with indignation the Embassy official asked me to remove that red and, hadn't I told him what I wished to remove from the lower parts of his body, he would have punished me without hesitation. Neither shall I ever forget what happened in the holy city of Qom where as a woman I was rejected from all the hotels, all the public places. To interview Khomeini I had to wear a chador, to put on the chador I had to take off my blue jeans, to take off my blue jeans I had to hide somewhere, and of course I could have done the operation in the car with which I had come from Tehran. But my interpreter begged me not to. «Please, Madame, please! For such a thing, in Qom, we could face death penalty». Refusal after refusal we then landed at the ex-Royal Palace, now the townhall, where a merciful guardian let us in. We got to a lavish lounge still furnished with a throne (the former Shah Reza Pahlavi's throne) where I felt like a Virgin Mary who shelters in the stable to deliver the Child, I locked the door and guess what happened. As the Koran forbids an unmarried couple to stay alone in a room, all at once the lavish lounge door opened wide. The mullah charged with the Morality Control burst in panting «shame-on-you, shame-on-you, this-is-a-sin, an ungodliness», and there was only one way to avoid being arrested for ungodliness: to get married. To sign the certificate of short-term marriage (four months) that he was nervously waving, and get married at once. The point is that my Joseph, I mean my interpreter, was already married. To a Spanish and Catholic girl, a certain Consuelo who was very jealous and consequently not ready to undergo the outrage of a second wife. As for me, I did not want to marry anybody. Even less so, the Iranian husband of a jealous Spanish and Catholic girl. At the same time, however, I did not want to be arrested and lose the interview with Khomeini. So I struggled with the dilemma do-I-marry-him-or-not, and...

You are laughing, I am sure. For you this is just a funny event. An anecdote. So I will not tell you the rest. I will leave you with the curiosity of knowing whether I married him or not, and to make you cry I'll recount you the story of the twelve impure men (what was the impurity they had committed I never knew) whom in 1975 the sons of Allah executed at Dacca, Bangladesh. They executed them in the stadium, with bayonet stabs in the thorax, and at the presence of twenty thousand believers who sitting in the tribunes prayed Allah-akbar, Allah-akbar. God-is-great, God-is-great... Oh, yes: I hear very well what you are thinking. The ancient Romans, you are thinking, those Romans of whom my culture is so proud, used to amuse themselves with watching Christians being eaten by lions. All over Europe the Catholics, those Catholics whose contribution to the History of Thought I acknowledge and respect, used to amuse themselves with watching the heretics burn alive. But a lot of time has passed by, in the meantime we have become a little more civilized, and even the sons of Allah should have understood that such things must not occur. Yet they do. After the impure young men they killed a ten-year-old child who in order to save one of the condemned, his brother, had thrown himself on the executioners. Don't-hurt-him, don't-hurt-him. They crushed his head with the heels of their heavy boots. And if you don't believe me, read over my reportage or the reportages of the French and German and British journalists who were there as well. Even better, look at the photographs taken by one of them. The German. Anyway the point I want to underline is that, as soon as the execution ended, the twenty thousand believers (many women) left the tribunes and came down to the ground. But not in a disordered, tumultuous way: in a proper, very solemn manner. They properly composed a cortege, a procession. They solemnly reached the scene of the carnage. And always praying their obsessive litany, Allah-akbar, God-is-great, Allah-akbar, they passed over the corpses. They reduced them to a carpet of crushed bones. They destroyed them like the Twin Towers.

Ah! I could go on and on and on, with these revolting stories. I could recount events I have never reported, never published. Because do you know what the problem is with people like me, I mean people who have seen too much? It is that at a certain point we get used to horrors. Reporting them makes us feel like chewing old cud and we keep that stuff for ourselves. On the cruelty of the polygamy recommended by the Koran and never blamed by the cicadas, I could recount for instance the case of Alì Bhutto: the Pakistani Prime Minister who was hung by his ultra-Moslem adversaries. I knew Alì Bhutto. To interview him, I stayed at his side for two weeks. And without any prodding one night, in Karachi, he told me the story of his first marriage. A marriage celebrated despite his despair («I don't want to marry, I don't») when he was less than thirteen years old. The wife, a beautiful cousin in her late twenties. He told it among tears. A tear slid down his nose then fell on his lips where he licked it sadly. Later, though, he changed his mind. He asked me to purge certain details. And I did because I have always had an enormous respect for people's privacy. Enemies and Heads of State included. Moreover, I have always felt an acute discomfort in listening to their private matters. (You should have seen the impetuousness with which once I interrupted Golda Meir who was disclosing to me how unhappy she had made her husband with her passion for politics. «Golda, are you sure you want to speak about this thing?»). But a couple of years later I met Bhutto again. I met him in a Rome bookstore, by chance. Both pleased with the fortuitous encounter we went to have tea, while having tea we started to talk about Islam, and all of a sudden he exclaimed: «I was wrong in asking you to purge the details of my first marriage. One day you should tell the whole story». And the whole story begins with the blackmail he had endured on the eve of the ceremony. That is, when he screamed I-don't-want-to-marry, I-don't. «If you do, we'll give you the roller-skates and the cricket-clubs you always ask for». It includes the wedding-reception in which the bride did not participate because a Moslem woman cannot take part in any reception, not even her own wedding one. It reaches its acme the night when the marriage had to be consummated but wasn't. «I did not even try. In spite of my looks I was really a boy, a child: believe me. I didn't know where to start from, and instead of helping me she cried. She cried, she cried. So I soon began to cry with her and then, tired of crying, I fell asleep in her arms. The day after I left Karachi to go and study in a London college. Therefore I saw her again only after my second marriage, when I was a grown up man and enamored with my second wife. I saw her in private, at her solitary Larkana house, and this time I felt attracted by her. She was still so beautiful... But how to explain it? I like women, you see. I hate chastity. Some consider me a lady-killer, and after that reunion we were together many

104

times. Yet from her I never had children. I mean, I never put myself in the condition to have children with her. The memory of the first night has always prevented me from exercising my husbandly rights and duties... And when I go to Larkana where she lives all alone and forgotten because, should she touch another man, she would become guilty of adultery and die lapidated, I feel ashamed of myself and of my religion. It is a despicable thing, polygamy. It is a despicable thing the arranged marriage. And no religion is as oppressive as mine».

(Well, Bhutto: it's done. Wherever you are, and too bad if you are only in your grave, be sure that the request you made in Rome has been honored. Poor soul, I did nothing for you when the military Junta of the monstrous general Zia overthrew your government and hung you inside that prison as a delinquent. How could I? But the whole story of your sad first marriage is finally told the way you wanted).

*   *   *

Now forget Alì Bhutto, forget the barbarian execution of the desperate boy and of the twelve young men in Dacca. Forget the mullah of the Morality Control and my marriage or not

105

marriage in Qom, forget my red nails' comic misadventure, and come with me along the road of contempt that Moslems have for us women. A contempt I have found even in circumstances during which it would be legitimate to expect a drop of human decency. In 1973, for example, I happened to experience it with a unit of Palestinian fedayins at that time hosted in Jordan by King Hussein: the only likable and civil leader whom, besides my hanged friend, I have known in the Islamic world. (So civil that when he wanted a new wife, he divorced. No polygamy. So likable that, when in the course of an interview I told him how hard it was for me to address a person with the words Your-Majesty, he cheerfully exclaimed: «Then call me only Hussein! A king's job is a job like any other»). And here is the example. One night the secret-base I was visiting as a reporter was hit by a fierce Israeli air-raid. Everyone started running towards the solid shelter provided by the cave of a mountain, and I did the same. But the commander stopped me. He said that having a woman side-by-side with his men would be obscene, then he ordered his aides-de-camp to place me somewhere else and guess where the bastards locked me up: inside a wooden and isolated hut which was a dynamite-deposit. I realized it only when I lit my lighter and saw the boxes stamped with the scary admonition

«Explosive-Danger-Explosive». However the worst doesn't stay in this detail. It stays in the fact that they did not lock me there by chance or mistake. They did it on purpose, to amuse themselves, as if my risk of blowing up for a nearby blast would be the most hilarious thing on earth. In fact, when the air-raid was over, they all satisfiedly guffawed: «We never had such fun».

I'll drive you along that road of contempt with a documentary recently made in Afghanistan by a smart newswoman from London. A documentary so appalling, so infuriating, so heart-rending, that it caught me unprepared even though the titles had put me on edge. «We warn our spectators. This program contains very disturbing images». Have you seen it? Has it been broadcasted in Italy? Whether it has or not, I tell you at once what the «very disturbing images» are. They are those that show the execution of three women in burkah, guilty of we don't know what. An execution which takes place in a square of Kabul, next to a desolate parking lot. And in this desolate parking lot a vehicle suddenly arrives. A little truck from which they are pushed outside. The burkah of the first woman is brown. The burkah of the second woman is white. The burkah of the third one is light blue. The woman with the brown burkah is clearly terrorized. She hardly stands up on her feet, she staggers. The woman with the white burkah looks like dazed. She proceeds with cautious steps as if she were afraid of falling and hurting herself. The woman with the light blue one, very short and very small, proceeds instead with resolute steps and at a certain point she halts. She makes the gesture of helping her companions, of encouraging them. But a bearded ruffian with the skirt and the turban intervenes, with violent shoves he separates them, he obliges them to kneel on the asphalt. The scene occurs while people pass by or eat dates or pick their noses, as idly and indifferently as if the forth-coming deaths had no importance whatsoever. Only a young man standing at the edge of the square watches with some curiosity. As for the execution, it takes place in a real expeditious manner. No military firing squads. No drums, no reading of some sentence. I mean, no ceremony or pretence of ceremony. The three women are kneeling on the asphalt when their murderer, another bearded ruffian with the skirt and the turban, emerges from nowhere with a machine-gun in his right hand. He holds it as if it were a shopping bag. Walking in an indolent and bored manner, as if killing women were a usual component of his daily life, he goes towards the three now motionless figures. So motionless that they no longer seem like three human beings: they seem like packages abandoned on the ground. He comes from behind their back, as a thief who slyly assails his victims. He joins them and without hesitation, catching us by surprise, he shoots point blank into the nape of the one with the brown burkah who immediately falls forward. Stone dead. Then, always walking in an indolent and bored manner, he moves to the left and shoots into the nape of the one with the white burkah who falls forward in the same way. Just on her face. Then he moves a little more, again to the left. He stops a little to scratch his genitals, he shoots into the nape of the small one with the light blue burkah who instead of falling forward remains for a long instant on her knees. Her bust upright, erect. Fiercely erect. Finally she collapses on her flank and, in a last gesture of rebellion, she raises the hem of the burkah to show a bare leg. But with icy imperturbability he covers it and calls the sextons. Leaving three large ribbons of blood the sextons grab the corpses by the feet, they drag them away, and the local Minister of Foreign Affairs plus Justice Mr. Wakil Motawakil appears on the TV screen. (Yes, I did take his name. Carefully... We never know what opportunities life can offer. One day I might meet him along a deserted road, and before doing what I dream of doing I might feel the scruple to check his identity. «Are you really Mr. Wakil Motawakil?»).

He is a thirty or forty-year-old piece of lard, this Mister Wakil Motawakil. A very stout, very bearded, very mustached piece of brown lard. He has the shrill voice of a eunuch and speaking of the three women's execution rejoices ecstatically. He wiggles like a pot of gelatin, he squeaks: «This is a very joyful day. Today our good city has regained peace and security». But he does not say in what way the three women have deprived the city of its peace and security. He does not mention the reason why they have been condemned and executed. Did they take off their burkahs, did they unveil their faces to drink a glass of water? Did they challenge the prohibition to sing, did they hum a lullaby to some newborn child? Or did they commit the crime of laughing? (Yessir: of laughing. I wrote «laughing». Didn't you know that Fundamentalist Moslems forbid women to laugh?). I am asking myself these questions, when Wakil Motawakil fades away and on the screen a saloon filled with pretty girls without burkah appears. Girls with unveiled faces, naked arms, low-cut dresses. And one curls her hair, another puts mascara on her eyes, another paints her lips and her nails red. While doing this they joke, they play, they laugh, so I decide that we are no longer in Afghanistan: the smart newswoman has returned with her troupe to London where the documentary is ending with a scene of relief and hope. Mistake. We are still in Kabul, and her voice sounds raspy. Strangled. With that strangled and raspy voice she whispers something, she kind of murmurs: «We are now in one of the most prohibited places of the city. A very clandestine, dangerous place. A hairdresser shop». Or so I hear because, with a shiver, all of a sudden I recall the harm that in 1980 I unwittingly did to a hairdresser of Tehran whose shop named «Chez Bashir-Coiffeur pour Dames» had been closed by the government as a place of perdition. Not considering the reason why it had been closed and exploiting the fact that he was a fan of mine, that he kept all my books translated in Farsi, I convinced him to open the shop. «Please, Bashir, please! Just half an hour. I need to wash my hair and in my room there is no hot water». Poor Bashir. Taking off the seals and letting me in the empty shop he trembled like a wet dog and repeated: «Madam, Madam! You don't understand the risk we are running. If someone surprises us here, if someone finds out, I go to jail and you too». Well, nobody surprised us while trembling like a wet dog he washed my hair. The concierge was keeping an eye on the door. But eight months later, when I went back to Tehran, (another ugly story I have never reported), I asked for Bashir and I was answered: «Don't you know? Someone found out and informed the Morality Control's authorities. After you left, Bashir was arrested for obscenity and still is in jail». I recall, yes, and I finally realize that almost certainly the three Kabul women have been executed because they had been to the hairdresser. I finally understand that they were three Resistants, three heroines, and tell me: is this the «culture» you talk about when you deferentially speak of Contrast-Between-the-Two-Cultures?!? No, my dear, no. As obsessed as I am with my cult of freedom, a while ago I wrote that in this world there is room for everybody. That my mother used to say the-world-is-interesting-because-it's-various. I also wrote all-the-worse-for-the-women-who-are-so-stupid-to-accept-their-slavery, the-important-thing-is-that-their-slavery-is-not-imposed-upon-me. But I was wrong. Dead wrong. Because I forgot that freedom separated from justice is half a freedom, that defending only our own freedom is an insult to justice. And apologizing as Pope Wojtyla does for his predecessors' Crusades, imploring the forgiveness of the three heroines of Kabul, of all the women executed tortured humiliated brainwashed by the Moslems, (brainwashed to the point of joining the procession in the stadium of Dacca), I declare that their tragedy concerns me too. It concerns each of us, cicadas included. And...

To the male cicadas, I mean the egoists who never open their mouth on this matter, never lift a finger against the burkah, I have nothing to say. The turpitudes that Moslem men commit on Moslem women do not concern their hypocritical interpretation of justice, and my suspicion is that they secretly envy Wakil Motawakil. Not seldom, in fact, they beat and abuse their wives. To the homosexual cicadas, the same. As devoured as they are by the wrath of being half and half, they abhor even their mothers. And in women they see only an egg to clone their uncertain species. To the female cicadas, on the contrary, that is to the Feminists of bad memories, I do have something to say. Take off your mask, you phony Amazons. Do you remember when instead of saying that my example was blazing your trail and demonstrating that a woman can do any work like a man, even better than a man, you vilified me with your insults? Do you remember when, instead of following my lesson you defined me «dirty-male-chauvinist-pig» and stoned me because I had written a book entitled *Letter to a Child Never Born*? («She has the brain in the uterus»). Well: where did your bitter, acrimonious feminism go? When did your supposed and flaunted belligerency end? Can you tell me why, when it comes to your Moslem sisters, to the women who are tortured and humiliated and assassinated by the real male-chauvinist-pigs, you imitate the silence of your little men? Can you tell me why you never organize a short barking in front of the Afghan or Saudi Arabian Embassy, why you never raise your voice against the turpitudes I speak about, why you keep silent even if they take place under your eyes? Have you all fallen in love with the enemy, with Mr. Bin Laden? Do you all dream of being raped by him? Or do you simply not give a damn for your Moslem sisters because you consider them inferior? In such case, who is a racist: you or me? The truth is that you are not even cicadas. You are and you have always been nothing but petulant chickens that can only flap in the coop. Cluck-cluck, cluck-cluck.

And now let me complete my point.

*   *   *

You know: when I despair and fight for our endangered freedom, for our culture threatened by the Wakil Motawakils and humiliated by their Western protectors, I don't always see only the apocalyptic scene with which I started this letter. The bodies that jump by dozens from the eightieth and ninetieth and hundredth floors, the first Tower that implodes and swallows itself, the second Tower that melts and liquefies as if it really were a stick of butter. Often those two gorgeous skyscrapers that no longer exist get superimposed by the two millenary Buddhas that the Taliban destroyed last Summer in Afghanistan. The four images mix, become the same thing, and I wonder: have people erased that shame from their mind? Well, I have not. In fact when I look at the two little brass Buddhas I keep on the fire-place of my living-room in New York, (a present that an old Khmer monk gave me in Pnomh Penh during the war in Cambodia), my heart wrings. And instead of them I see the two enormous ones that, imbedded inside the solid rock, overlooked the valley of Bamiyan. The valley that, thousands of years ago, each caravan coming from the Roman Empire and going to the Far East or vice versa used to pass through. The cross-road where the legendary Silk Route, amalgam of every culture, used to run. I see them because about them I know all what I should. That the oldest one, (Third Century A.D.), was thirty-five meters tall. The other one, (Fourth Century A.D.), fifty-four. That both of them had their back welded to the rock and were covered with polychrome plaster. A symphony of red and yellow, green and blue, brown and violet. That their faces and their hands were golden, therefore in the sun they shone like gigantic jewels. That the niches' interior, now as empty as empty orbits, contained frescoes of exquisite workmanship. That until the arrival of the Taliban even the colors had remained intact...

My heart wrings because for works of art I have the same veneration that Moslems have for the tomb of the Prophet and his Koran. To me a work of art is as sacred as Mecca is for them, and the more ancient it is the more sacred it becomes in my eyes. Besides, every object of the Past is sacred to me. A fossil, a parchment, a worn coin. Any testimony of what we were and we did. The Past arouses my curiosity more than the Future, and I shall never tire of sustaining that Future is only a hypothesis. A probability, a supposition, thus a non-reality. At most, a hope that we try to embody with our dreams and fantasies. The Past, on the contrary, is a certitude. A concreteness, an established reality, a school that we cannot do without because if we don't know the Past we don't understand the Present and we cannot try to influence the Future. To embody it with our dreams and fantasies. Besides, any object which has survived the Past is precious in my eyes because inside itself it brings an illusion of eternity. It represents a victory over Time which decays and kills and nullifies, it ignites the hope that defeating Death is possible. And like the megalithic marvel of Stonehenge, like the Minoic palace of Cnossos, like the Pyramids with their Sphinx, like the Parthenon, like the Coliseum, like a centenary turtle or a millenary tree, for instance a majestic sequoia of Sierra Nevada, the two Buddhas of Bamiyan gave me all this. But those criminals, those Wakil Motawakils, destroyed them. They slaughtered them.

My heart wrings also for the lucid way in which they slaughtered them. For the cold awareness and the pleasure with which they committed the infamy. Because, remember, they did not act in an impetus of madness, in a sudden and temporary outbreak of insanity. That is, with the irrationality of the Maoists who in 1951 destroyed Lhasa and like drunken buffalos broke into the monasteries then in the Dalai Lama's palace, burnt the millenary parchments, smashed the millenary altars, tore up the millenary vestments, fused all the golden or silver Buddhas: shame on them ad saecula saeculorum amen. The ignominy of Lhasa, in fact, was not preceded by a trial and by a verdict. It did not have the characteristics of an execution carried out on the basis of juridical or supposedly juridical norms. Moreover, it occurred unbeknown to the world. In the case of the two Bamiyan's Buddhas, instead, there was an authentic trial. An authentic verdict, an execution based on juridical or supposedly juridical norms. There was a conscious and premeditated crime, a conscious and calculated iniquity carried out while the whole world begged: «Please don't. We implore you, don't. The archaeological monuments are a universal heritage and the Bamiyan's Buddhas don't harm anybody». Oh! Even the United Nations and the neighboring countries, Russia and India and Thailand and China (which had on its conscience the sin of Lhasa) joined the petition. But the verdict of the Islamic Supreme Court of Kabul was pronounced all the same: «Every pre-Islamic statue will be destroyed. Every pre-Islamic symbol will be wiped out. Every idol condemned by the Prophet will be pulverized». It was pronounced on the 26th of February 2001 (not 1001), that verdict. The same day in which the Taliban regime authorized the public hangings in the stadiums, and the last Women's Rights were withdrawn. (The right to laugh, the right to wear high heeled shoes, the right to stay at home without black curtains at the windows, among the others). Then the havoc began, and remember the machine-gun shots on the Buddhas' faces? Remember the noses that flew away, the chins that disintegrated, the cheeks that dissolved, the hands that crumbled? Remember the press conference that the Taliban Minister Qadratullah Jamal gave to the foreign journalists? «We are having a hard time in demolishing them. The grenades and the fifteen tons of explosives we placed at the feet of the two idols have not been sufficient. Heavy artillery, neither: we have only succeeded in damaging their heads. So we are now counting on the help of a friendly country, on the assistance of an expert in demolition, and in three days the sentence will be fully carried out». (Which was the friendly-country: Saudi Arabia or Pakistan? And who was the expert in demolition? Ousama Bin Laden himself?). Finally, the real and double execution. Those two thunderous bursts. Those two dense clouds. They resembled the clouds that six months later would erupt from the New York Towers. And I thought of my friend Kon-dun.

*　*　*

Because, you see, in 1968 I interviewed an adorable man. The most peaceful, the most tolerant, the wisest man I ever met in my life of wanderer. The present Dalai Lama. The monk that Buddhists call Living Buddha. He was thirty-three years old at that time. Not much younger than me. And, for the past nine years, a pope without church, a king without kingdom, a god in exile. As such he lived in Dharamsala, a town at the foot of the

Himalayas and almost on the border that separates Kashmir from Pradesh, where the Indian government hosted him along with a few thousand Tibetans escaped from Lhasa. It was a very weird, unforgettable encounter. Now drinking tea in his small villa brightened by the white mountains and the silvery glaciers as pointed as knives, now walking in a green meadow filled with scented roses, we remained together from early morning to late night. He, to talk. I, to listen. Oh, the young god had realized at once that I was a woman without gods. Those almond-shaped eyes made more sagacious by the gold-framed lenses had observed me well at my arrival. Yet he kept me a whole day, in his boundless liberality he treated me as if I were an old friend or a girl to flirt with. At a certain point he even paid me the nicest homage I have ever received by a man. Under the pretext that the heat was unbearable, he went to change. He took off the precious cashmere stole which covered his naked torso, and put on a light T-shirt with the image of Popeye. The cartoon character. The odd sailor who always holds on to the pipe with his teeth, always eats canned spinach to grow stronger. And when in laughing disbelief I asked where he had found such a crazy garment, why he had put it on, he seraphically answered: «I bought it at the New Delhi market and I put it on to please you».

The interview was a waterfall of incredible stories. About his childhood sadly spent with books and teachers, to begin with, so that at six years old he already studied Sanskrit and astrology and literature. At ten, dialectics and metaphysics and astronomy. At twelve, the art of ruling as a pope. As a king. About his adolescence gloomily spent in the effort to become a perfect monk, to control the temptations, to stifle the desires, and only cheered by a little garden where he raised gigantic cabbages. «One meter in diameter, eh?». About his love for mechanics and the fact that, could he have chosen a job, he would have become an engineer not certainly a monk. Even less, a Dalai Lama. «In the palace garage I had discovered three old automobiles which had been sent as a gift to my predecessor. Two 1927 Baby Austin, one blue and one yellow, and a 1931 orange Dodge. They were very rusty, but I made them go and even learnt how to drive them in the palace courtyard. Only in the palace courtyard because at Lhasa we had no roads. Just pathways and mule-tracks». He also told me about Mao Tse Tung by whom, at eighteen, he had been invited and practically sequestered for eleven months. («I let him do it because I thought that my staying in Beijing would save Tibet, but... Poor Mao. You know, there was something pitiful, pathetic, in Mao. Something that aroused in me a sort of tenderness. He always had dirty shoes and bad breath, he always smoked one cigarette after another, and he always talked of Marxism. Only once did he change the subject and admitted that my religion was a good religion. He never said stupidities, anyway»). He also told me about the atrocities committed by the Maoists at Lhasa, and about his flight from Tibet. The flight of a twenty-four-year-old who disguised as a soldier leaves the sacked palace, mingles with the terrorized crowds then reaches the capital's suburbs where he steals a horse and, chased by a Chinese airplane, runs for life. He hides in the caves and runs. He flattens under the bushes and runs. Mountain after mountain and village after village he finally arrives at Dharamsala, but what for? Now his subjects are scattered in India or in Nepal or in Sikkim, after his death it will be practically impossible to find a successor, and almost surely he is the last of the Dalai Lamas. Oh... his voice broke when he said that almost surely he was the last of the Dalai Lamas. So I interrupted him, I asked: «Your Holiness, can you really forgive your enemies?». And instead of answering yes or no he looked at me in disbelief, astonishment. Then he took breath and shouted: «Enemies?!? I did not, I do not, consider Maoists as enemies! I do not have enemies! A Buddhist cannot have enemies!».

To Dharamsala I had arrived from Vietnam, remember? And that year in Vietnam I had been through the Tet Offensive, the May Offensive, the siege of Khe Sanh, the bloody battle of Hue. In other words, I came from a world of incurable hate. A world where the term enemy-ennemi-nemico was pronounced every few seconds, had the same sound of our hearts' beat. So, in hearing that passionate shout «I-do-not-have-enemies, a-Buddhist-cannot-have-enemies», I lost my usual detachment. And I almost fell in love with that young monk. With his almond-shaped eyes, his Popeye T-shirt, his goodness, his soul. When I left I said that I hoped to see him again, I gave him my telephone numbers, and I was pleased to hear his answer: «Of course. On condition that you no longer call me Your Holiness. My name is Kon-dun». But I never saw him again except on TV where I noticed that he was aging like me... Apart from the day when a friend brought me his regards, («the Dalai Lama asked me to remind you that his name is Kon-dun»), I never heard from him either. Our lives ran along such different directions, such opposite paths... On the wake of that encounter, on the nostalgia of that day, however, during these thirty-three years I have read a lot about Buddhism.

And I have found out that, contrary to Moslems and their «an-eye-for-an-eye-a-tooth-for-a-tooth», Buddhists really refuse the term «enemy». I have found out that at no time did they proselytize through violence, at no time did they make a territorial conquest under the pretext of religion, at no time did they conceive the principle of Holy War... Some scholars deny it. They say that Buddhism is not that pacific, that mild, and to support their theory they give the example of the Buddhist warriors who lived in Japan many centuries ago. Nevertheless they too concede that not even the Buddhist warriors ever fought to wage a Holy War, to make proselytes. And it is a fact that Buddhism's history does not register any Ferocious Saladin or any Leone IX, any Urban II, any Innocentius II, any Pius II, any Julius II, I mean popes leading armies and slaughtering people in the name of God. Yet Moslems persecute Buddhists too. They blow up their millenary statues, they forbid them to practice their religion, they convert them by force. Thus I ask: who is next, now that the «idols» of Bamiyan have been blown up like the Twin Towers? The other Unfaithful who pray Vishnu or Shiva, Brahma, Krishna, Annapurna? The Indians who live in Kashmir, that is, in the disputed region that Pakistan wants to occupy since 1947 Partition? In other words: do they hate only the Christians and the Buddhists, these voracious sons of Allah, or do they aim to subjugate our whole planet?

The question remains even if Ousama Bin Laden dies or converts to Catholicism. Or if his disciples become as liberal as my Kon-dun. Because Ousama Bin Laden and his disciples, I shall never tire of repeating, are only the most recent manifestation of a reality to which the West has been stupidly or cynically shutting its eyes for centuries. For God's sake! In 1982 I did see them destroy the Catholic churches, burn the Crucifixes, soil the Madonnas, urinate on the altars, transform the chapels in latrines. I did see them unleash their contempt for the other religions. I did see them in Beirut. That Beirut which until their arrival had been so rich, so happy, so elegant, and which today is a squalid copy of Damascus or Islamabad... That Beirut where the Palestinians had been accepted by the Christians like my Kon-dun's Tibetans had been accepted by the Indians at Dharamsala, and where they had immediately installed themselves as masters. Where under the leadership of Mr. Arafat they had built a State inside the State then spread all over Lebanon. Read the newspapers of twenty years ago, if you don't recall. Or read again my *Inshallah*. It is a novel, agreed, but based on historical events that thousands of people have experienced and hundreds of journalists have reported in every language. Memory may fade, hypocrisy may win, but History cannot be cancelled... It can be ignored or forgotten, yes. It can be falsified as Big Brother does in Orwell's novel, but it cannot be cancelled. And, always speaking of those who pretend to ignore or to forget: how come the so-called leftists no longer mention Karl Marx's warning «Religion is the opium of the people»? How come they never open their mouth against the theocratic regimes of the Islamic countries? Think over: not one Islamic country is governed by a democratic regime, by a laical regime. Not a single one. Even those which are crushed by a military dictatorship like Iraq and Libya and Pakistan, even those which are subdued to an absolutist monarchy like Saudi Arabia and Yemen, even those which are ruled by a more reasonable monarchy like Jordan and Morocco, never stray from the path of a religion that controls and regulates and tyrannizes every moment of its victims' existence. (A small example? The late King of Morocco, often seen as a modern guy, never revealed the name and the face of his first wife: the queen. And the fact that the present one has given the name plus the photo of the girl he married is considered a sign of modernity). Come on, then! Can such regimes cohabit with our principles of freedom, of democracy, of civilization? Can we condone them in the name of broadmindedness and lenience and understanding and pluralism? If so, why did we fight Mussolini and Hitler then Stalin and company? Why did we go to Vietnam? Why did we oppose that unbearable Fidel Castro and still do? Why did we throw bombs on Milosevic's Yugoslavia? Why do we act as policemen of the world and kill and die in wars declared against the enemies of freedom, of democracy, of civilization? Are these principles valid in certain cases only, with certain countries only? Aren't Islamic tyrannies as unacceptable and inadmissible as the fascist and communist ones? Enough with your duplicity, your ambiguity, your hypocrisy, cicadas of every country and language! Cut the bullshit and answer: where did your laicism, your secularism, your trumpeted liberalism go? Better: did it ever exist? Because, if it ever existed, if in some corner of your bad conscience it still exists, I nail you with another question. With what right do you condemn the orthodox Jews who wear the black hat like the Amish and grow beards like Ousama Bin Laden and curl their hair in ringlets like La Dame aux Camélias?!? That right belongs to me who am a free spirit, a laic, a person who refuses any form of tyranny or religious interference, who doesn't even want to hear the term Theocratic State! Not to you.

127

And now let's talk of the pioneers who have established their bridgeheads, their settlements, in my country. In my city.

*　*　*

I do not go to erect tents at Mecca. I do not go to recite Paternosters and Avemarias in front of the Prophet's tomb. I do not go to urinate on the walls of their mosques. Even less, to defecate on them. When I am in their countries, (something from which I don't derive any kind of pleasure), I never forget that I am a guest and a foreigner. I pay attention not to offend them with clothes or gestures or behaviors which are normal for us but unacceptable for them. I treat them with dutiful respect, dutiful courtesy, concern. I apologize if out of ignorance or lack of attention I break some of their rules or superstitions. And, when in my memory the two blown up skyscrapers mix with the two blown up Buddhas, I also see the image (not apocalyptic but for me equally symbolic) of the enormous tent that two summers ago disfigured the Cathedral Square of Florence. My city.

An enormous tent erected by Somali Moslems (Somalia is a country with deep connections to Ousama Bin Laden, remember, and also the country where in 1993 seventeen Peace Force Marines were slaughtered then maimed) to blame the Italian government that for once hesitated to renew their passports and to accept the hordes of their relatives. Mothers, fathers, brothers, sisters, uncles, aunts, cousins, pregnant wives, and possibly the relatives of their relatives. A tent erected next the Archbishop Palace on the sidewalk on which they used to leave the shoes and the bottles of water with which they washed their feet before the prayer. Therefore placed in front of the Santa Maria del Fiore Cathedral and a few steps from the Baptistery. A tent furnished like a small apartment: tables, chairs, chaise-longues, matelas to sleep and to fuck, ovens to cook and to stink up the square. Therefore open to every show. A tent equipped with electricity plus enriched by a tape playing the voice of a muezzin who continuously exhorted the Faithful, reproached the Unfaithful, injuriously suffocated the beautiful sound of the bells. And, along with all this, the yellow streaks of urine that profaned the millenary marbles of the Baptistery as well as its golden doors. (Good Heavens! They really take long shots, these sons of Allah! How could they succeed in hitting so well that target protected by a balcony and more than two yards distant from their urinary apparatus?). With the yellow streaks of urine, the stench of the excrements that blocked the main entrance of San Salvatore al Vescovo: the exquisite Romanic church (Ninth Century) that stands near the square and that the sons of Allah had transformed into a latrine like the churches of 1982 Beirut. You know.

You know because it was I who called you and asked you to intervene on your newspaper: remember? I also called the Mayor of Florence who immediately paid me a visit, humbly endured my fury, shyly admitted that my protests were legitimate. «You are right. Really right». But he did not remove the tent. He forgot or, better, he lacked the guts. I also called the Minister of Foreign Affairs who was a Florentine speaking with a very Florentine accent, and who had the power to authorize or deny the renewal of the foreign passports. And he too endured my fury. He too admitted that my protests were legitimate. «You are right. Really right». But he didn't do a thing to remove the tent. Like the Mayor, he forgot. Or, better, he lacked the guts. Then, (more than three months had elapsed), I changed my tactics. I called the policeman who ran the City's Security Office and barked: «Dear policeman, I am not a politician: when I say something, I really mean it. If by tomorrow you don't remove the damn tent, I burn it. I swear on my honor that I burn it, that not even a regiment of soldiers could prevent it. And for this I want to be arrested. Handcuffed, locked in jail, arrested! So the newspapers and the TV stations will report that Fallaci has been incarcerated in her own city for defending her own city. And this will throw shit on all of you». Well... being more intelligent than the others, within a few days the policeman removed the damn tent. All that remained in its place was an immense and disgusting stain on the square's pavement. Meaning, the filthy residues of the three and a half months' horrid bivouac. But mine was a poor victory, a Pyrrhic victory, indeed. It was because, immediately afterwards, the Somali passports were renewed by the Minister of Foreign Affairs with the very Florentine accent, and all the Somali requests were accepted by the government. Today the protesters and their fathers, their mothers, their brothers, their sisters, their uncles, their aunts, their cousins, their pregnant wives (who in the meantime have given birth) are all settled where they wanted to settle. I mean, in Florence and in other cities of Europe. It was a poor and Pyrrhic victory also because the removal of the tent did not change the various outrages that for decades have been humiliating the city that was the capital of art, of culture, of beauty. And because the incident did not dishearten the other Moslem intruders. The Albanians, the Sudanese, the Bengalese, the Tunisians, the Egyptians, the Algerians, the

Pakistanis, the Nigerians, who fervidly contribute to the commerce of drugs. (Apparently, a sin not condemned by the Koran). With them, the pedlars who infest our streets and squares to sell fake watches or pencils. The steady vendors who expose their merchandise on little carpets placed on the sidewalks. The prostitutes who ply their trade and spread Aids even along the country roads. The thieves who assault the country houses, especially at night, and don't you dare face them with a revolver because in such case you are the one who goes to jail. (Along with the accusation of racism, of course).

Oh, yes. All of them are where they were before my policeman removed the tent. The steady vendors squat even inside the splendid courtyard between the two arcades of the Uffizi Galleries. The Vasari Courtyard. They even block up the access to the museums and to the libraries. For instance, the ancient Laurentian Library (the one that preserves treasures like the millenary Vergilian Code or the Middle Ages' illuminated texts) and the glorious National Library. They also occupy the area surrounding the Tower of Giotto, the span of the Ponte Vecchio (Old Bridge) where they encamp in front of the jewelry shops, and the sidewalks bordering the Arno river. My lovely Lungarni... They also lodge on the ultra-centenary churches' parvises. For instance the parvis of San Lorenzo Basilica. The spot where publicly disobeying the Prophet they get drunk, and when drunk they harass women. (Last Summer they even harassed me who am by now an antique lady. And it goes without saying that they heavily paid for their effrontery. One is still moaning over his genitals). The pretext, of course, is selling their merchandise. But by «merchandise» they mean leather goods fabricated on models protected by a patent, thus illegal. They mean posters, postcards, cheap watches, African statuettes that illiterate tourists believe to be Renaissance sculptures. And, I repeat, drugs. «Je connais mes droits, I know my rights» a Nigerian drug-vendor hissed to me in French when I threatened to have him arrested. And his were the same words that two years before, in Porta Romana Square, an extremely young son of Allah had pronounced after lasciviously grasping my breast and inevitably receiving a fierce kick in the genitals. «I-know-my-rights». They also request, and obtain, to be financially supported by the municipality. They also demand, and obtain, the construction of new mosques. They who in their countries don't even let the Christians build a tiny chapel, and who so often slaughter the nuns or the missionaries. And woe betide the citizen who protests, who exasperatedly boasts: «Go exercise your rights in your own countries». Woe betide the passer-by who walking amongst the «merchandise» tramples on a bag or a poster or a statuette. «Racist, racist!». Woe betide the policeman who approaches them to ceremoniously ask: «Mr. Steady Vendor, Your Excellency, please, would you care to move your stuff just a inch and let people walk?». They eat him alive. They bite him like vicious dogs. At the very least they insult his mother, his father, his ancestors, his progeny. And the Florentines keep their mouths shut. Intimidated, resigned, blackmailed by the word «racist». They don't even react if you bawl out the rebuke that, during Fascism, my father used to yell at the cowards who accepted the Black Shirts bullyings and brutalities: «Haven't you a drop of dignity, you vile sheep?!? Haven't you a little self-esteem, you base rabbits?».

It happens in any other Italian city: true. It happens in Turin, for instance. That Turin to which we owe so much for the Unification of Italy, and which today does not even look like an Italian city: it looks like an African one. (By the way: Turin's walls are particularly smeared with the Moslem inscriptions that read: «Get off. This street is mine»). It happens in Venice. That Venice where the thousand pigeons of San Marco Square have been chased away by the pedlars and by the steady vendors, and where the millenary monuments are soiled by the same urine streaks that soiled the Baptistery of Florence. It happens in Genoa. That Genoa where the wonderful palaces ecstatically admired by Rubens are now inhabited by pitiless vandals and die like beautiful women raped by herds of wild boars. It happens in Rome. That Rome where certain vandals don't even respect the archeological sites. And where the politicians of every color and falsehood protect them to obtain their future vote. (Yes, now our politicians even speak of granting our guests the right to vote). And where, not satisfied with the apologies for the Crusades, the Pope incessantly blesses them. (Once again, Holy Father: why don't you come to your senses? Why in the name of the Unique God, don't you lodge those brothers of yours inside the capacious Vatican? Provided that they don't shit in the Sistine Chapel too, of course. That they don't urinate on the statues of Michelangelo too, that they don't soil the paintings of Raffaello too). It also happens in Switzerland, in France, in Belgium, in Germany, in Spain, in England, in Holland, in Sweden, in Norway, in Denmark, in Hungary, in Greece, etcetera etcetera amen. It happens all over Europe. But in Italy this scandal surpasses all limits of decency, endurance. Because in terms of artistic patrimony our cities have more to lose than any other European city. And because Italy is so desperately near to Albania, to Bosnia, to Egypt, to Libya, Tunisia, Algeria, Morocco: the countries from which the overwhelming majority of those invaders comes... Do I need to remind you that Italy is practically an island at the mercy of Moslem countries' emigration, a long bridge stretched in the middle of the Mediterranean, a land of 5.281 miles of uncontrollable coasts? Do I need to remind you that almost all the emigrants leaving Albania and Bosnia and Egypt and Libya and Tunisia and Algeria and Morocco and the rest of Moslem Africa travel by sea, that even if directed to North Europe they land on our coasts? Do I need to remind you that once landed on our coasts they find such an excess of hospitality that instead of going further at least the 25 per cent of them stop in Italy, settle in Italy like the Moors settled in Portugal and in Spain one thousand years ago?

Now it is I who do not understand. Because, dammit, their abetters and protectors call them «foreign workers» or «the-manual-labor-we-need». And many of them do work, it's true. Italians have become so dandy. They go on holidays to the Seychelles, they spend Christmas in Paris, they have English speaking babysitters, and they feel ashamed to be laborers. They all want to be doctors, professors, generals, admirals, land-owners, pop singers, entrepreneurs. They no longer want to be associated with the proletariat, and for Christsake: in a society someone must take care of the work which requires physical fatigue... But the intruders I have just described, what kind of laborers are they? In what way do they provide the manuallabor that the Italian ex-proletariat does not provide anymore? Loafing around the cities with their «merchandise», their prostitutes, their drugs? Disfiguring our monuments, lounging on the parvises of the ancient churches? Getting drunk in spite of the Koran, whispering obscenities to the antique ladies or grasping their breasts, hissing I-know-my-rights? Something else, then, I don't understand: if they are as poor as their abetters and protectors claim, who gives them the money to come? Where do they find the five or ten thousand dollars per head that pay for the trip? Might it be that this money is supplied by some Ousama Bin Laden for the mere purpose of establishing the Reverse Crusade's settlements and better organizing Islamic terrorism? Might it be that the five or ten thousand dollars per head are lavished by their wealthy sheiks for the purpose of materializing a conquest that is not only a conquest of souls but also a conquest of territory? They breed too much. Italians don't produce babies anymore, the idiots. For decades they have had and still have the lowest birth-rate in the West. Our «foreign workers», instead, breed and multiply gloriously. At least half of the Moslem women you see in our streets are pregnant or surrounded by streams of children. Yesterday, in Rome, three of them delivered in public. One in a bus, one in a taxi, one along the street. No, this story does not convince me. And those who don't take it seriously are as wrong as the fools who compare this migratory-wave to the migratory-wave which hit America in the second half of the 1800s and in the first quarter of the 1900s. Let me stress you why.

* * *

Time ago I heard one of the innumerable ex-Prime Ministers who have pestered Italy in the last decades say on TV: «My uncle too was an emigrant. I well remember my uncle who left for America with his cardboard suitcase». Absolutely not, my misinformed or insincere ex-Prime Minister. Apart from the fact that you cannot have had an uncle going to America with the cardboard suitcase because the uncles with cardboard suitcases went to America in the first quarter of the 1900s, that is, when you were not yet born, it is not the same thing at all. And it is not the same thing at all on

138

account of reasons you ignore or pretend to ignore. Here they are.

Number One: America is a continent of 3 million and 618.770 square miles. Its surface still has vast regions that are totally uninhabited or so scarcely inhabited that in many cases you can go for months and months without seeing a person pass by. And, especially in the second half of the 1800s, those regions were still empty or almost empty. No cities, no towns, no roads, no houses: at most, a little fort or a corral to change the horses. The majority of the population, in fact, was concentrated in the Eastern States. In the Midwest there were only a few audacious adventurers and the tribes of the Native Indians, of the so-called Redskins. In the Far West, even less: the Gold Rush had just started. Well: Italy is not a continent. It is a rather small country, thirty two times smaller than America, and overcrowded: around 58 million Italians versus 282 million Americans. Therefore, if three or four hundred thousand sons of Allah settle in Italy every year, (as they do), for us it is as if three or four million Mexicans settled in Texas or in Arizona or California every year. Number Two: for one century, that is from the war of Independence until 1875, America was an open frontier. Its borders and coasts were unguarded, strangers could come at their will, and immigrants were more than welcome. To grow and flourish the newly born nation needed to exploit its available space, its potential richness, and just because of this on the 20th of May 1862 Abraham Lincoln signed the Homestead Act. The Act which gave away 270 million acres of federal land. In Oklahoma, for example. In Montana, in Nebraska, in Colorado, in Kansas, in the two Dakotas... An Act, moreover, which did not benefit the Americans only. With the exception of the mistreated Chinese and of the persecuted Native Indians, anybody (man or woman) could claim and obtain 160 acres as a gift. The conditions were to be no younger than twenty-one, to settle for no less than five years, to transform the wild place into a farm with a house, to raise a family and (if the claimer was not American) to ask for citizenship. Following the slogans «American-Dream», «America-Land-of-Opportunities», in fact, many claimers came from Europe. They came in such number that whole tribes of Natives (Cherokee, Creek, Seminole, Chickasaw, Cheyenne) were brutally kicked out and ignominiously closed in the reservations. Well, in Italy there has never been a Homestead Act inviting strangers to settle in our territory. «Come, strangers, come. If you come, we give you a nice piece of land in Chianti or in Val Padana or in the Riviera.

For you we kick out the Natives, meaning the Tuscans and the Lombards and the Ligurians, we place them into some reservation». As in the rest of Europe, all the immigrants who grieve Italy have arrived on their own initiative. With the damn boats, the damn rubber dinghies of the Albanian mafia, and despite our coastguards trying to push them back. Because we are not an open frontier, my dear ex-Prime Minister and supposed nephew of the uncle with the cardboard suitcase. We have no land to give away. No empty regions to populate. No Cherokee or Creek or Seminole or Chickasaw or Cheyenne and so on to kick out.

Number Three: not even America-Land-of-Opportunities went on being as lenient as it had been until Lincoln's presidency. In 1875, for example, the American government realized that some limits had to be set, and the Congress issued a law denying entry to ex-convicts and prostitutes. In 1882, a second one that banned the lunatics and those who would likely become a public burden. In 1903, a third one which excluded epilectics and professional beggars and contageously ill plus anarchists. (The improper name which at that time was given both to the nuts who assassinated presidents and to the radicals who promoted turmoils or strikes). From that moment on, the Immigration policy became very restrictive, and illegal immigrants were expelled on the spot. In Italy, in Europe, instead, they enter at their wish and pleasure. Terrorists, thieves, rapists. Ex-convicts, prostitutes, beggars. Drug-dealers, contageously ill. Not even those who have a work-permit undergo any background check. Once landed, they simply are lodged and fed and cured at the expenses of the Natives. I mean of the Italian taxpayers. They even receive a monthly amount of money for little expenses. As for the illegal ones, if by chance they are expelled because they have committed some outrageous crime, they come back. If they are expelled again, they come back again. To commit other crimes, of course. While politicians do nothing. Damn! I shall never forget the rallies with which, last year, the illegal ones filled our squares to impudently demand the residence-permits. (Often raising their national flags or the red flags). Those nasty, distorted faces. Those fists ready to hit us Natives, to throw us in some reservation. Those howls that resurrected the howls of Khomeini's Iran and Bin Laden's Indonesia, Malaysia, Pakistan, Iraq, Senegal, Somalia, Nigeria, etcetera... I shall never forget because, besides being offended, I felt mocked by the politicians who said: «We would like to expel them, to repatriate them.

But we do not know where they hide». Hide?!?
You miserable jerks! They were thousands and
thousands, in those squares, and did not hide at all.
To expel them, to repatriate them, it would have
been enough to surround them with a few armed
policemen and soldiers. To load them on trucks, to
take them to an airport or a harbor, and send them
back to their countries.

As for the final reason, my dear ex-Prime
Minister and supposed nephew of the uncle with
the cardboard suitcase, it is so simple that even a
half-witted baby would comprehend it. America is
a very young country. If you think that its birth
as a nation took place at the end of the 1700s, you
conclude that today (year 2002) she is only a
couple of centuries old. It is also a nation of immigrants. Since the Mayflower, since the thirteen colonies, since always, everybody in America is an immigrant. Or the child, the grandchild, the far or
near descendant of an immigrant. As a nation of
immigrants, she is the most incredible, strong blend
of races and religions and languages ever existed
on this planet. As a very young country, she has a
very short history. Thus, her cultural identity is not
well defined as yet. Italy, on the contrary, is a very
old country. With the exception of Greece, I would
say, the oldest in the West. Her recorded history

dates back three thousand years, that is, since Rome was founded. Better, since the Etruscans were already a civilized society. In these three thousand years, and in spite of the Roman Empire, in spite of the invasions that ultimately caused the fall of that extraordinary achievement, in spite of the occupations that dismembered us for centuries, she has never been a nation of immigrants. That is, a blend of races and religions and languages. She hasn't even melted with her subduers. All foreigners who occupied and dismembered us (Germans and Scandinavians and Spanish and French and Austrians) have never been capable of changing our entity. In return, they have been absorbed by us as water sucked up by a sponge. (Just to get an idea, think of the Hasbourg-Lorraines who in 1735 became the rulers of Tuscany and settled as grandukes in Florence where their dynasty lasted until 1859. That is, until the Unification. They soon called themselves Tuscans, Florentines. Like Florentines they spoke, they wrote, they behaved... One by one they forgot to be Austrians and, when in Vienna to visit their relatives, they whined: «I miss my Tuscany, I miss my country!». And the identical thing occurred with the Bourbons who ruled Naples, the Kingdom of the two Sicilies. They forgot to be Spanish, they became Neapolitans). As a result, our cultural identity is well defined. And though it contains some elements that the sponge sucked up, (consider our many dialects, our many habits, ways of eating) in no way does it include the Moslem world. In no way has it been influenced by it. Moreover, for two thousand years our entity has been based upon a religion called Christianity. Upon a church called Catholic Church... Take me as an example. «I am an atheist, I am an anticlerical, I have nothing in common with the Catholic Church» I always say. And it's true. But it is also untrue. Because, whether I like it or not, I have a lot in common with the Catholic Church. Damn, if I do! How couldn't I? I was born in a landscape of domes, monasteries, Christs, Madonnas, Saints, crosses, bells. The first music I heard when I came into this world was the music of the bells. The Santa Maria del Fiore Cathedral's bells that at the Time of the Tent the muezzin's voice injuriously suffocated with his Allah-akbar. In that music, that landscape, that Church to which even great minds like Dante Alighieri and Leonardo da Vinci and Michelangelo and Galileo Galilei bent, I have grown up. Through it I have learnt what sculpture and architecture and painting and poetry and literature are, what beauty combined with knowledge is. Thanks to it I began to ask myself what is Good, what is

Evil, if God exists. If He invented us or we invented Him, if the soul is a chemical formula that can be analyzed in laboratories or something more. And by God...

See? I wrote «by God» again. With all my laicism, my anticlericalism, my atheism, I am so imbued with Catholic culture that Catholic culture makes part of my written and spoken language. By-God, for-God, thank-God, good-Heavens, Good Lord, my Lord, Holy Jesus, Virgin Mary, Christ here, Christ there, for Christsake... These expressions come so spontaneously to me that I am not even aware of pronouncing or writing them. And shall I say it all? Although I never forgave Catholicism for the infamies it imposed on me starting with the fucking Inquisition that in the 1600s also burned my foremother Ildebranda, poor Ildebranda, the music of the bells caresses my heart. I like it so. I also like those beautifully painted Christs and Madonnas and Saints. In fact I collect old icons. I also like abbeys and cloisters and monasteries. They give me an irresistible sense of serenity and I often envy those who live inside. Besides, let's face it: our Cathedrals are more beautiful than the mosques and the synagogues and the Buddhist temples and the bleak Protestant churches. My family cemetery is a Protestant cemetery.

146

It accepts the dead of any religion, true, but it is a Protestant cemetery. One of my great-grandmothers was Waldensian, one of my great-aunts was Evangelic. The Waldensian great-grandmother, I never knew her. She died young. The Evangelic great-aunt, yes: I knew her. When I was a little girl, she used to take me to the religious services at her church and what a bore! I felt so weary with those people who did nothing but chant the Psalms, with that priest who was a pastor, not a priest, and did nothing but read the Bible. I felt so dreary in that church which did not seem like a church and only contained the pews plus an enormous cross. Not a Jesus, not a Madonna, not an angel, not a saint, not a candle, a silver, and no incense. I even missed the stink of the incense, and I would have given a lot to be in the nearby Basilica of Santa Croce where those things existed in plenty. The things, the symbolic frills, which belonged to my life. To my culture. You know, in the garden of my Tuscany country-house I have a minuscule old chapel. It is always closed, alas. Since Mother died, nobody cares for it. So, when I go home, I open it. To dust the altar, to see if some mouse has made a nest or eaten some page of the missal. And despite my laicism, my atheism, there I feel at my ease. Despite my anticlericalism, there I feel at peace. (And

I bet that the majority of the Italians would confess you the same. To me it was confessed, good Heavens, by Enrico Berlinguer: the Secretary General of the then Italian Communist Party, the man who set on the historical compromise between the marxists and the Catholics...).

For Christsake, and here we go again, I am saying that we Italians are not in the same conditions as the Americans. We are not their melting pot, their mosaic of diversities glued together by a citizenship. I am saying that just because our cultural identity has been well defined for thousands of years we cannot bear a migratory wave of people who have nothing to do with us... Who are not ready to become like us, to be absorbed by us like the Hasbourg-Lorraines of Tuscany and the Bourbons of Naples. Who, on the contrary, aim to absorb us. To change our principles, our values, our identity, our way of life. And who in the meantime molest us with their retrograde ignorance, their retrograde bigotry, their retrograde religion. I am saying that in our culture there is no room for the muezzins, for the minarets, for the phony abstemious, for the humiliating chador, for the degrading burkah. And should that room exist, I wouldn't give it to them. Because it would be like deleting our identity, like nullifying our accomplishments.

148

Like spitting on the freedom that we have earned, on the civilization that we have installed, on the welfare that we have achieved. It would be like selling my country, my patria. And my country, my patria, are not on sale. Which drives me to the point I want to clear up once and for all.

* * *

I am Italian. They're mistaken those who think I am American. I never asked for American citizenship. When the American ambassador in Rome Maxwell Rabb asked me why I didn't take it on the basis of Celebrity Status, I answered as follows. (And I still see his piercing eyes intensely observing me while I'm talking, his forehead that frowns, his lips that smile now sadly and now amusedly). «Mister Ambassador, Sir: I am profoundly linked to America. I am so even though I often quarrel with her. Even though I condemn her flaws and mistakes and faults. Her too frequent oblivion of the noble principles on which she was born and grew up, to begin with. Her childish cult of opulence, her inconsiderate waste of richness, her moral hypocrisies, her bullish arrogance in the financial and military field. (An arrogance that inevitably emerges and has always emerged from a country arrived at her level of power and supremacy, by the way). And also the haunting memory of a plague now fully wiped out and sometimes erroneously exploited by its victim's descendants, in my opinion, but too long endured. The plague of slavery. Also her paucities in education, I mean the gaps that impoverish her knowledge because let's admit it: scientifically and technologically her knowledge is superb. In the humanistic domain, instead, it is kind of inadequate. Also her constant glorification of violence and brutality, a glorification that especially through the movies poisons her rescued but unlearned plebes and contaminates the rest of the world. Also her sordid and obsessive exhibition of sex, her boring deification of homosexuality, her immoderate and boundless hedonism. All faults that contributed a lot to the fall of the Roman Empire and one day will lead to her fall: remember. Nevertheless, I am profoundly linked to her. America is for me a husband, a lover, to whom I shall always remain loyal and faithful notwithstanding his defects. (And provided that he does not cuckold me with some unforgivable betrayal). I care for my husband, my lover. I like his impudence, his courage, his optimism. I adore his geniality, his ingenuity, his trust in himself and in the future. I compliment the respect he has for common people and for the wretched, the ugly, the dejected. I envy the infinite patience with which he bears the offenses and the slanders. I praise the marvelous dignity and even humility with which he faces his incomparable success, I mean the fact that in only two centuries he has become the absolute winner. The archetype that both in the Good and in the Evil we all want to follow or to imitate. The lifebuoy to which we all resort or ask for help. And I never forget that, hadn't this husband defeated Hitler, today I would speak German. Had he not held back the Soviet Union, today I would speak Russian... Finally, I admire his undisputed and indisputable generosity. For instance the one he shows when I arrive in New York, I hand him my Italian passport with the U.S. Residence-Card, and the Customs Officer says: "Welcome home". It seems to me such a fine gesture of unselfishness, bounteousness. It reminds me that America has always been the Refugium Peccatorum, the orphanage, of the people without a country. Without a patria, without a home, a mother. But I already have a country, dear Ambassador Rabb. I already have a patria, a home, a mother. My patria, my home, my mother, is Italy. I love my mother more than I love my husband and in taking the American citizenship I would feel as if I were repudiating, disavowing, her».

I also said to him that Italian language is my language. That in Italian I write, that in English I only translate myself. And with the same effort of when I translate myself in French. Which means, sensing it as alien. Familiar yet alien. Finally, I told him that the fact of listening to the Mameli Hymn, my country's national anthem, moves me immensely. Each time I hear those words Brothers-of-Italy, Italy-has-woken-up, taratà-taratà-taratà, I get a lump in my throat. I don't even notice that it is not a great piece of music and that it is always played badly. I only think: it is the hymn of my Patria, of my Mother. Each time I see the Italian flag, the same. And listen: in my Tuscany country-house I keep a nineteenth-century tricolor which looks like a rag. It's all torn up, all eaten up by mice, and stained with spots of blood. Blood from some combat, I believe. But though it carries the Savoyard crest, that is, the symbol of a monarchy not dear to me, (I only acknowledge that without Vittorio Emanuele II of Savoy, the first King of Italy, we could not have reunited the country), I treasure it like a jewel. Crest or not crest, we died for that rag. For that tricolor. Right? We died hung, shot, decapitated, killed by the Austrians, by the Popes, by the Dukes of Modena, the Bourbons. We also made the Risorgimento with it. We also fought the Wars of Independence for it, and does anybody realize what the Risorgimento was?!? It was the revival of a dignity lost to centuries of invasions and humiliations! It was the resurrection of a pride that for centuries had been frustrated by all the foreigners who had vilified us! Does anybody comprehend what our Wars of Independence were?!? They were much more than the War of Independence was for the Americans, by God! Because the Americans had a single enemy to fight: England. We had all the enemies that the Congress of Vienna had restored on our soil after splitting us like a roast chicken, instead! Does anybody understand what the Unification of Italy was, how many tears we shed for it?!? When they commemorate their victory over England and raise their flag and sing «God Bless America», Americans put their hand on their heart. On their heart! We commemorate nothing, we put our hand on nothing, and thank Heavens if someone doesn't place it I don't say where!

For that tricolor we shed blood and tears in the following century too: remember? I do. Because for it in 1848 my maternal great-great-grandfather Giobatta faced the Austrians at Curtatone and Montanara, was horrendously disfigured by one of their rockets and ten years later was bestially cudgeled by their Leghorn jailers. Still young, he became a limping wreck: yes. But from 1914 to 1917, my paternal uncles fought the First World War in the trenches and on the mountains of Carso. And during the Second World War my father fought in the Resistance, was arrested as well as tortured. The whole family joined his struggle and at fourteen I did too. In the «Justice and Freedom» Corps, a branch of the Italian Army's Volunteers for Freedom, with the codename Emilia. And one year later, when the Italian Army discharged me as a simple soldier, I felt so proud. So elated. I had been fighting for my flag, Good Lord, for my country! For my flag, for my country, I had been an Italian soldier! In fact, when I was told that as discharge I would receive 15.670 liras, I didn't know whether to accept them or not. It seemed to me so unfair to receive 15.670 liras for having performed my duty. Then I did accept them. None of us in the family had a decent pair of shoes, so with that money I bought shoes for me and my little sisters. (Father and Mother, no. They refused).

* * *

Of course my Italy, the Italy for which I never took the American citizenship and said to Ambassador Rabb what I said, is none of today's Italies. To begin with, the Italy of the Italians who (like the other Europeans, let's clear it at once) take side with the Ousamas Bin Ladens and their Palestinian admirers. I mean the Italy of the Italians who in order to shake hands with a third-class Hollywood star would sell their daughter to a Beirut brothel and yet, when thousands of New Yorkers are reduced to ashes, scornfully giggle and snear: «Good. Americans got it good». Or the Italy of the Italians I described with regard to their soccer-games and their lack of patriotism. Or the Italy of the opportunists, of the turncoats, who scream with the same enthusiasm God-save-the-King and God-save-the-Republic, Hail-Mussolini and Hail-Stalin. Hail-Whoever-passes-by. Or, even worse, the Italy of the red and black Fascists who force me to recall the tragic remark made by the writer Ennio Flaiano as soon as democracy was restored. «Italian fascists divide in two categories: the Fascists and the Anti-fascists». Oh, please! Do you want me to list all the Italies that are not my Italy, that make me suffer and at times curse my loyalty to the Mameli Hymn, to the blood-stained flag I keep in Tuscany?

Alright. I will. Because like the Englands, the Frances, the Germanies, the Spains and so on, I mean like the whole of today's Europe, those Italies are strictly connected with the Reverse Crusade. With the blindness, the deafness, the laziness, the stupidity, the masochism which prevents the West (a certain America included) from seeing the chasm inside which we risk tumbling down. And here they are... The Italy of the ex-Communists who for fifty years (I was extremely young when it all began) filled my soul with bruises, to begin with. Who tormented me with their illiberality, their pretentiousness, their contempt for anyone who was not a Communist. (Every non-Communist was labeled by them with the terms reactionary or troglodyte or servant-of-the-Americans, «Americans» written «Amerikans»: remember?). Who treated me like an Unfaithful but after the Berlin Wall's dismantlement immediately changed their attitude and, as lost as chicks no longer hidden under the wings of the brooding hen called Soviet Union, pretended to renegate their past. To play the role of liberals. In fact now they behave as if that wall had been demolished by them, and love to be called «goodists». An extravagant term which derives from the word «good», and to which I oppose the more realistic term goody-goody. They also love to name their party and their alliances with floral or vegetable terms. Oak-tree, Olive-tree, Daisy. And instead of a hammer-sickle's symbol they display the sketch of a donkey, that is, of an animal unused to show intelligence. Instead of going to Moscow or to Beijing, they come to New York and buy their shirts at Brooks-Brothers.

Their sheets, at Bloomingdale's. Instead of insulting the Americans, they celebrate conventions with an American slogan that sounds like the advertisement of a detergent: «*I care*». And never mind if the laborers who used to wave the rivers of red flags, the lakes of red flags, do not speak English. Never mind if my carpenter, who is an old and honest Communist, does not understand what «*I care*» means. Never mind if he reads it «Icare» and thinks that Icare is Icarus, the mythological character who wants to fly but his waxen-wings melt under the sun, and all confused, lost, he asks me: «Fallaci, what in the hell does Icarus have to do with them?». Never mind if I must tell him that Icarus has nothing to do with them and their Goodist Convention, that «*I care*» does not mean «Icarus»: it means «I-am-interested-worried-concerned». Never mind if at this point the good man gets angry and yells: «Who are the fucking idiots who invented this fucking stupidity?!?». Now they don't even call me reactionary, troglodyte, servant-of-the-Amerikans. They even avoid to mock and deride me as they did during the war in Vietnam and particularly in 1969 after my reportage from Hanoi. But here I must open a parenthesis that I really own to myself.

Parenthesis. Seduced by the articles I had written in 1967 and in 1968 from South Vietnam, articles which fully expressed what I thought about that questionable war, in 1969 the Ho Chi Minh government invited me to visit North Vietnam. So I went and it did not take me long to conclude that the rascals of Hanoi were no better than the rascals of Saigon: Stalinism and Maoism reigned there much more than in the Soviet Union and Popular China. Using the same independence of judgement in which I had reported the war from Saigon, I therefore denounced this truth. (Something that nobody, at that time, dared to. Read the stuff written by the journalists who made my identical experience, and you'll see that none of them dared to. None). I denounced it, of course, through the daily miseries that common people lived in. For instance, the fact that they were obliged to piddle and defecate separately. A procedure which permitted the Agricolture Ministry to collect the human excrement untouched by urine then transform it into a fertilizer, a torment for which you could be controlled while piddling and defecating. (Thanks to my female escort, An Thi, I was controlled twice. Once in my hotel bathroom, once in the field. And I let you imagine my reaction to such an intrusion). I denounced it also through the wickednesses they imposed on those who did not belong to the Communist Party. Especially on the Catholics and on the Buddhists who fought side by side with the Vietcong without being party's members. And to better explain the unknown reality I wrote what an old Vietminh, a Dien Bien Phu veteran, had whispered to me while bursting in tears: «Madame, madame, vous ne savez pas comme nous sommes traités ici! Madam, Madam, you do not know how we are treated here». As a consequence, when the reportage appeared, a Communist magazine of Rome reacted with a serial of attacks which portrayed me as a high society's idiot. And do you remember the despicable title which, spread on two pages and in enormous capital letters, at each issue summarized my idiocy? «La signorina Snob va in Vietnam. Miss Snob goes to Vietnam».

Not as despicable, though, as the defamations that a young actress from Hollywood (whose name I don't mention out of contempt) spewed on me after a trip which followed mine and occurred while my reportages were driving the Hanoi leaders crazier than An Thi during my staying there. Led by her scarce intelligence as well as by her presumptuousness and love for publicity, in fact, once back home the young actress gave several lectures and slandered me by saying what those Hanoi leaders had asked her to say. That I was sold to the American government, that I had gone to North Vietnam to spy on behalf of the Pentagon, that

I belonged to the CIA and had written those false-hoods under the CIA's direction. I did not kill her, alas. I limited myself to send her a short and ferocious letter in which I said that history and politics were too serious matters for nullities of her kind, and in which I promised to kick her cute behind at the first occasion. But the occasion never came. I was always engaged in the too serious matters, mainly some war, and she was always engaged in some marriage or movie or video that teached how to stay in good shape. Thus, I keep my promise now. And instead of kicking her cute behind I spit in her face as I do with Bin Laden's admirers. Better: as forgiveness is not a virtue of mine, I use these pages also to express my disdain for one of the two American prisoners I met in Hanoi· the bomber-pilot who was released after the fuss I caused with my interview... A meeting which took place in front of several North Vietnamese officers and began with his humble picking up the candies that the cruelest of them threw to him on the floor. At each candy, a double and profound bow of thanks. An interview (taped) during which he kept repeating how well he was treated by his jailers who even fed him «with excellent meat-loaf». In fact I uselessly tried to resurrect his dignity with the revelation that Americans had just been on the Moon, and when the encounter was

160

over I had a tremendous quarrel with the officer who threw the candies. A quarrel for which I was forced to leave Hanoi before my visa expired. Yet, when released, the poor guy did not show me a drop of gratitude. He declared that what I had written (and published in *Look magazine* as a cover-story) was a total lie. No candies thrown on the floor, no humble and double bow to thank the bastard in uniform, no praises for the («excellent») meatloaf. No attempt of mine to resurrect his dignity with the revelation of the American voyage to the Moon. In his displaying as a hero, he even insinuated that I was a Commie. Well... He was Lieutenant R.F. Frishman. Parenthesis closed.

I know: evil doesn't hold any passport. Human beings do not need to murder thousands of people in the name of Allah to prove it. And now that I have finally taken my triple revenge, let's go back to the goody-goodies who have imitators even among the bomber-pilots and the Hollywood stars. I mean the Italian cicadas. No: they no longer insult me as they used to. (Tomorrow, however, they will again: be sure). They don't, and everybody has forgotten that they did. But I have not. And full of bitterness, impotence, sadness, I roar: «Who gives me back those fifty years of bruises on my soul, of outrage to my honor?». One day I put this question also to an ex-militant of the ex-Communist Youth Federation. The employment agency (as I call it) from which most of the leftist Mayors and Officials and Congressmen who afflict our country come. I reminded him that Fascism is not an ideology, it is a behavior, and asked: «Who gives me back those fifty years?». As by now he too plays the liberal, I expected an apology. «Please, forgive us, please». On the contrary, he sneered and answered: «Why don't you sue us?». Words from which I deduce that really the leopard never changes its spots. And thanks to which I confirm that their Italy is not, never will be, my Italy.

* * *

It is not the Italy of their opponents either. In fact I do not vote for their opponents. As a matter of fact, I don't vote for anybody. And I confess the second thing with anguish. With grief, with big sense of guilt. Because also the non-vote is a vote. A legal vote, a legitimate vote. A vote to say to-hell-with-you-all. But at the same time it is the most tragic vote that exists. The gloomy vote of a citizen who doesn't trust anybody, doesn't identify himself with anybody, doesn't know how to be represented by somebody, and consequently feels abandoned defrauded alone. As alone as I am. Oh,

I suffer so much when our elections' time arrives! I do nothing but curse and smoke, in those days, and between one curse and another, one cigarette and another, I moan: «God! We went to jail, we died tortured executed exterminated in the concentration camps, to regain the vote. And I do not vote...». Yes, I moan and I execrate the rigor that prevents me from voting. I moan and I feel envy for those who are capable of compromising, of adapting, of entrusting their hopes to somebody who seems less bad than the others... (When there is a referendum, instead, I vote. Because in a referendum I don't have to deal with men or women by whom I refuse to be represented: the democratic process takes place without intermediaries, then. «Do you want the monarchy?». «Not at all». «Do you want the republic?». «Of course». «Do you want the hunters shooting next to your house?». «Hell, no». «Do you want to see your privacy protected by Law?». «Hell, yes»). And now that this point is cleared up, let me address a few words to the leader of those opponents. I mean, to the present Prime Minister of Italy.

Dear Prime Minister of Italy, I know that while listening to what I think about the ex-Communists you swell with joy, you gloat like a happy bride. But don't be impatient. I have it in for you too. I made you wait so long, I kept you on tenterhooks till now, because you don't belong to my fifty years of sorrows. Because in that sense you are absolutely innocent. And because I don't know you so well as I know the goody-goodies. You're such a recent acquisition, Sir, such a novelty. Just at the very moment when I was deciding that I no longer wanted to hear about politics, (a holy word for me, as you may have realized) you appeared. You sprouted in its Olympus the same way an unspecified plant sprouts in a field, so we confusedly look at it and wonder: «What's that? A radish, a nettle?». Since then I have been observing you with curiosity and perplexity, without deciding if you are a radish or a nettle yet thinking that if you are a radish you are not a great radish and if you are a nettle you are not a great nettle... Besides, you too seem to nourish such doubt: at least with your mouth, (with your eyes much less), you smile or laugh too much. Even when there is no reason to smile or to laugh, I mean, when we should cry, you smile or laugh as if you did not take yourself too seriously. As if you knew that your sudden success in politics is an extravagant and undeserved quirk of chance, a farce of history, a bizarre adventure of your life. Which is one of the reasons why I don't like you. And here are the others, Sir.

To begin with, your shortage of good taste and acumen. For instance, the fact that you want to be called Cavaliere. Cavalier. Why? It is not an important title, believe me. Italy produces more Cavalieri than Turncoats. Just think that once, in that crowd, a President of the Republic wanted to insert me too. To prevent the disaster I had to spread the word that if he dared to do such a thing I would sue him for slander. Yet you display it like ex-aristocrats display their feudal crests and blazons. Well... Considering that Mussolini too loved being a Cavaliere, that title seems to me a political error mingled with a funny ostentation. And a Head of State cannot afford the luxury of political errors mingled with funny ostentations. If he does, he ridicules the country. Secondly, I don't like the tactlessness and the superficiality with which you have chosen the name of your party: Forza Italia, Go Italy. A name that evokes the screams of the stadiums' ruffians during the international soccer-games. Such mistake offends me as much as the Communist perfidies I just spoke about. Maybe even more, if I think that this time the bruise is not inflicted on me: it's inflicted on my country. Sir, you have no right to use the name of my country for your political party: my country is the country of all the Italians, also of your rivals and opponents and enemies. And even less have you the right to identify it with the damn screams of the damn soccer-games. For such an abuse my great-great-grand-

father Giobatta would have challenged you to a
duel with his sword of Curtatone and Montanara.
My uncles, with their bayonets of the Second
World War. My father would have broken your
nose, my mother would have gouged your eyes. As
for me, each time I see that name, my blood boils.
Who in the hell suggested it to you? Your valet,
your cook, your chauffeur?

I also dislike the lack of composure you
show with your habit of telling jokes. I hate jokes.
God, do I hate jokes. And I think that a Head of
State should not tell jokes, should not make politics telling jokes. Dammit, don't you know what
the word «politics» means?!? Don't you know where it comes from? It comes from the Greek noun
πολιτική which means Science of the State, Art of
Governing, Art of Administrating the Destiny of a
Nation. Something that does not go with jokes. It
does not, and believe me: when I hear yours, I suffer more than I do when I listen to the mellifluous
tarantellas of your French colleague Chirac. I lose
heart, I groan: «Christ! Doesn't this man understand that Italians voted for him out of despair,
that they accepted him only because they could
not stand his predecessors, I mean only because
they were sick and tired of being mocked by the
Left? Doesn't he understand that he should light a
candle to the Holy Virgin, behave like a serious

person, appear worthy of the fortune that befell him?!?». Finally, I don't like most of the allies you have chosen: the Green Shirts of the coarse separatist who doesn't even know what the colors of the Italian tricolor are, and the descendants of the ruffians who used to wear the Black Shirts. They say that they are no longer Fascists, those weird guys, and who knows: it might even be true. But I don't trust those who descending from the Communist Party say that they are no longer Communists, so why should I trust those who descending from the Fascist Party say that they are no longer Fascists? And having cleared all this, let's face the real problem.

I wonder if you have noticed, Mister Cavaliere, that I don't reproach you for your wealth. I don't align myself with demagogues who see in your wealth an unforgivable fault. In my opinion, denying a wealthy man the right to be a Prime Minister and govern a country is undemocratic. Illogical, illegal, and undemocratic. It is also profoundly imbecile because, as my companion Alekos Panagulis used to say, when a leader is very rich he does not need to steal. (Besides, also the overcelebrated Kennedys were and are considerably rich. The Bushes are far from being poor, and the Clintons still do every effort to increase their capital). I don't even reproach you for possessing a famous soccer-team and various TV channels. Your soccer-team doesn't bother anybody but me who cannot stand the screaming crowds, and as for the channels that spread or do not spread your political opinion, well... For decades your opponents have been controlling the media to the point of intellectual terrorism. Like in France and Germany and England, their way of manipulating the public opinion through newspapers and TV has been (and still is) so indecent, so intolerable, that they should keep their big mouths shut. No: the main fault that at this stage I reproach you for has nothing to do with that stuff. It's the one that follows. I have just read that, albeit grossly and inadequately, you preceded me in the defense of the Western Culture. But, as soon as the cicadas yelled racist-racist, you retracted at the speed of light. You spoke of unfortunate blunder, involuntary mistake, you promptly presented your apologies to the sons of Allah, then you swallowed the affront of their refusal and meekly accepted the hypocritical reprimands of your European colleagues plus the scolding by Blair. In short, you got scared. And this isn't right, Sir: no. In your place, I would have eaten them all alive with the mustard and Mr. Blair would not have dared to say to me what he said to you. (Do you hear me, Mr. Blair? I did praise you and I praise you for standing up to

Ousama Bin Laden as no other European leader has done. But if you play the worn-out games of diplomacy and shrewdness, if you separate the Bin Ladens from the world they belong to, if you declare that our civilization is equal to the one which imposes the chador and the burkah, then you are no better than the Italian cicadas. If you don't defend our culture, my culture and your culture, my Leonardo da Vinci and your Shakespeare, if you don't stand up for it, then you are a cicada too and I ask: why do you choose my Tuscany, my Florence, my Siena, my Pisa, my Uffizi, my Tyrrhenian Sea for your summer vacations? Why don't you rather choose Riyadh or Kabul, the desolate deserts of Saudi Arabia or the sinister rocks of dreary Afghanistan? I had a bad feeling when my Prime Minister received your scolding. The feeling that you will not go very far with this war. That you will withdraw as soon as it will no longer serve your career interests).

Unless, Mister Cavaliere, your retraction took place for the sake of that big-nosed tycoon with kaffiyeh and dark lenses who bears the ominous name of His Royal Highness Prince Al Walid: high member of the Saudi Royal Family and, I am told, your business-associate. Your Uncle Scrooge. Because in such a case I remind you that at least half of the Saudi Royal Family is accused of financing the Islamic terrorism. I remind you that several members of the Saudi Royal Family are involved in the Rabita Trust. The so-called charitable-institution that the American Ministry of Treasury has put on the black list of Bin Laden's supporters, and about which the same President Bush has spoken with manifest alarm. I remind you that most of them have at least one little finger in the Muwafaq Foundation, the other «charitable-institution» which transfers funds to Bin Laden. I remind you that in Saudi Arabia it is not the Law that commands: it is the Royal Family with its hundreds of Uncle Scrooges. I also remind you that twenty years ago, when the Palestinians used to kill us Europeans on the airplanes and in the airports, it was those Uncle Scrooges who financed the responsible, the craftsman, of that terrorism. I mean, Arafat. Finally I remind you that by will of the Royal Family the Saudi Ministry of Religion is in the hands of the most extremist Fundamentalists, the same ones who educated Ousama Bin Laden, and do you know what the so-called Saudi Ministry of Religion is? It is the mighty organism that divulges Fundamentalist theories throughout the world. That throughout the world builds mosques and schools where the unlucky Moslem students learn nothing but the six thousand and two hundred and thirty-six Koran's verses by heart. (Not a spark of history, geography, arithmetic, general knowledge: just verses to learn by heart). And where they are recruited to fight the Holy War. An operation which originated twenty years ago in Chechnya with the tragic results we all know, and which now is conducted especially in the African Continent. I remind you, Sir, and the suspicion that you retracted your inadequate defense of the Western culture for the sake of your business-associate infuriates me madly. It scandalizes me deeply, it forces me to repeat what your adversaries say: governing a country is not the same as possessing various TV channels and a soccer-team. To govern a country one must be equipped with qualifications that your Italian predecessors have never or almost never shown and that your European colleagues show even less, agreed, but that for sure you have not inaugurated. I speak of the values that characterize the real leaders in times of emergency. People like Klemens Lothar prince of Metternich, for instance, or Camillo Benso count of Cavour, or Benjamin Disraeli, or Winston Churchill, Theodore Roosevelt, Charles De Gaulle. Total lack of personal greed, intelligence, coherence. Passion, credibility, outstanding class, great style, and courage. Above all, much courage. Or do I ask too much?

Maybe yes. Especially on the matter of courage, I ask too much. The fact is that I have the right to be that demanding, Sir. I have it because, contrarily to you, I grew up in a very unusual wealth: the one that comes from having been educated like Bobby and Mayor Giuliani. I did, and to explain what I mean now I give you the example of my mother. Oh, Mister Cavaliere, you can't imagine who my mother was. You can't suppose what kind of teaching she gave to her daughters. (All daughters. No son). When during the Spring of 1944 my father was arrested by the nazifascists as a leader of the Resistance in Tuscany, nobody knew where they were holding him. The authorities refused to reveal it, and the Florentine newspapers only said that he had been arrested because he was a grim criminal hired by the enemy. (Read Anglo-Americans). But Mother said: «I shall find him. I swear». She went looking from prison to prison then at Villa Triste, the place where interrogations took place under torture, and here she succeeded in reaching the office of the chief. An Army Major called Mario Carità. Major Carità admitted that yes, he was the one holding the grim criminal Edoardo Fallaci, and contemptuously added: «Madam, you can dress in black. Tomorrow morning at six your husband will be executed at the Parterre. We waste no time with trials». Well, I always asked myself how I would have reacted in her place. And the answer has always been: «I don't know». But

172

I do know how Mother reacted. (Besides it is a well renowned story, alas). She remained for an instant totally motionless. As immobile and silent as if she had been struck by lightning. Then, she raised her right arm. She pointed her index finger toward Mario Carità and with a firm voice, addressing him as if he were a serf at her orders, she coldly said: «Mario Carità, tomorrow morning at six I shall do what you say. I shall dress in black. But if you are born from the womb of a woman, tell your mother to do the same. Because your day will come very soon».

As to what happened later, I'll tell you another time. For the moment it's sufficient to inform you that Father was not executed, that Mario Carità ended up exactly as Mother had announced, and that your Italy is not my Italy.

*   *   *

Nor is it the sluggish and flabby one that the consumer society softens with its abundance and the American hedonism fosters with its example. I mean the one that lives in the cult of enjoyment, comfort, pleasure, and by Liberty means Licentiousness. The one that ignores the concept of discipline or better self-discipline and consequently does not connect it with the concept of freedom, does not understand that freedom is also discipline or better self-discipline... The one that on his deathbed my father described with the following words: «In Italy we always speak about Rights and never about Duties. In Italy we ignore or pretend to ignore that every Right carries inside itself a Duty, that those who don't perform their duties do not deserve any rights». And also the one that derives from this. I mean the one of the young people who have a thirty thousand dollars car and travel the world and speak three or four languages but do not know the grammar, for instance. Thus, when they send you a postcard from Disneyland or Shanghai or Bombay, you find it filled with shameful mistakes of orthography. The one of the University graduates who have never heard of the Consecutio Temporum (Sequence of Tenses) nor of history. Thus they make monstrous errors of syntax or confuse Mussolini with Rossellini-the-husband-of-Ingrid-Bergman, Tchaikovsky with Trotsky, Napoleon with a famous cognac. And thank God if through some movie a couple of them have realized that in reality the famous cognac was a general then an emperor who lost at Waterloo and died in Saint Helena. So, please, do not ask them who our Founding Fathers were. If you mention Mazzini or Garibaldi or Cavour, they react with lightless eyes or pendulous tongue. Nor do I feel better because here it happens the same. (To verify what the young Americans know about their country's history, last night a famous Talk Show's host stopped a few specimens in the street. He asked an eighteen-year-old loafer of New York when Jefferson was born, what his achievements had consisted in, and the blockhead answered: «Jeff who? The baseball player?» He asked a twenty-four-year-old girl who introduced herself as a school-teacher what the Civil War had been, and the irresponsible fool answered that the Civil War had been a war against England. That the Confederates were guys of the North. The Unionists, guys of the South).

In return, those young Italians know how to fill themselves with drugs. How to waste their Saturday nights in the discotheques, how to wear blue jeans that cost more than a laborer's monthly salary. And like the Ivy League students who maybe know a little more about Jefferson and the Civil War but totally ignore who was Bismarck or what happened at Sebastopol or why the First World War exploded, why the Republic of Weimar collapsed, they also know how to exploit their parents in avoiding work. Like the anti-globalization rioters of Seattle and Stockholm and Genoa etcetera, they also know how to hide their faces under ski-masks to play the heroic guerrillas in times of freedom and democracy. The contemptible mollusks. The phony revolutionaries. The heirs of the 1968 charlatans who wanted to destroy the capitalistic world and now rule the Milan Stock Exchange or double their money in Wall Street. And these things disgust me in the most depressing manner because Civil Disobedience is a serious matter, not a pretext to have fun and become rich. Prosperity is a conquest of civilization, not a pretext to scrounge a living. And because I never played that trick. My parents, even less so. I started working when I was sixteen, dammit. My father, when he was only nine. My mother, when she was ten. And before dying, at sixty-four, she said: «I am happy to leave seeing that today's children do not work like adults, that they go to school and attend university». Poor mother. She believed that an obligatory school and a university accessible to everybody (two marvels she had never dreamed of) would drive young people to learn what she had not learned and would have loved so much to learn. She felt victorious. Good for her she died before realizing that she had lost, that we have lost again. Yes, lost. Because instead of learned young people we have donkeys with University degrees. Instead of future leaders we have mollusks with expensive blue jeans and phony revolutionaries with ski-masks. And do you know what? Maybe this is another reason why our Moslem invaders have such an easy game.

As for the Italy of the cicadas with whom I started this desperate letter and who after this desperate letter will hate me even more than they used to... Those supposed liberals who degrade and dishonor the meaning itself of the word liberalism. Those supposed Christians who profane and desecrate the meaning itself of the word Christianity. Those insects who disguised as ideologists, journalists, writers, actors, commentators, psychoanalysts, priests, warbling crickets, putains à la page, (that is, polished sluts), only say what they are asked to say. What helps them to enter or remain in the pseudo-intellectual jet-set and exploit its advantages, its privileges. Those parasites who have replaced the Gospels and the Marxist ideology with the fad of the «Politically Correct»... The fad or rather the hoax that in the name of Brotherhood (sic) preaches pacifism at any cost and repudiates even the war we fought against the nazifascism of yesterday. The fad or rather the fraudolent mockery that in the name of Humanitarianism (sic) reveres the invaders and slanders the defenders, absolves the delinquents and condemns the victims, weeps for the Taliban and curses the Americans, forgives the Palestinians for every wrong and the

Israelis for nothing. The fad or rather the demagogy that in the name of Equality (sic) denies merit and success, value and competition. In denying them it places on the same level a Mozart symphony and a hideousness defined «rap», a Renaissance palace and a tent in the desert. The fad or rather the insanity that in the name of Justice (sic) abolishes legitimate words and calls the road-sweepers «ecological operators», the housekeepers «family-assistants», the school-janitors «non-teaching personnel», the blind «visually-impaired», the deaf «audio-impaired», the crippled «foot-impaired». And homosexuality, «diversity». Homosexuals, «gays». (So that in speaking or writing you can no longer use the word «gay» to mean joyous or lighthearted. If you do it, they accuse you of embezzlement). The fad or rather the hypocrisy, the shit, that calls «local tradition» the infibulation. I mean the bestial practice by which, in order to prevent them from enjoying sex, Moslems cut young girls' clitoris and sew up the large lips of the vulvas. All that remains is a tiny opening through which the poor creatures urinate, and imagine the torment of a defloration... The fad or rather the farse that in Italy worships a Moroccan scribbler who pompously claims that the Western culture discovered Greek philosophy through the Arabs, that the Arab language is the Language of Science and the most important in the world, that Jean de La Fontaine did not write his «Fables» after Aesop, inspired by Aesop, but after reading certain Indian tales translated in French by an Arab guy named Ibn al-Muqaffa.** The fad, finally, which permits the cicadas to exploit at their own convenience the term «racism». They do not know what it means, yet they handle it with such wanton impudence that it sounds useless to quote the lapidary judgement given by an Afro-American: «Speaking of racism in relation to a religion not to a race is a big disservice to language and to intelligence». It sounds useless because, when invited to reason, cicadas react like the idiot of Mao Tse Tung's proverb: «If you point at the Moon with a finger, the idiot looks at the finger and sees the finger. Not the

---

** *Author's note*. I am referring to the individual whom the UN Secretary, Kofi Annan, has generously honored with a prize which has something to do with peace. And who slanders me declaring that my dislike for Islam is due to the mortifications or letdowns I have had with Arab men. (In a sentimental and sexual sense, of course). Well... To this individual I reply that, thank God, I never had any sentimental or sexual or friendly rapport with an Arab man. In my opinion there is something in his brothers of faith which repels the women of good taste. I also reply that his vulgarity fully demonstrates the contempt that Moslem men vomit on us women. A contempt that once again I reciprocate with all my heart and my brain.

179

Moon». And if by chance they see the Moon, it's the same. Because not having the guts that takes to go against the current, against the intellectual terrorism of the goody-goodies, against their conformism, they pretend to see the finger.

Now tell me, my dear, tell me: are these the people with whom you would like me to deal when you disapprove of my locked door? Now I'll put a chain on my locked door! I'll buy a mastiff with a good set of teeth and thank God if on the gate that precedes the door I fix a placard with the warning «Cave canem. Beware of the dog». Do you know why? Because I heard that some de luxe cicadas will soon come to New York. They will come on holiday, to visit the new Hercolaneum and the new Pompeii, I mean the Towers that no longer exist. They will take a de luxe airplane, they will choose a de luxe hotel, and after a de luxe drink they will immediately go to enjoy the ruins. With their very expensive cameras (two or three thousand dollars each) they will photograph the remains of the melted steel, they will snap suggestive images to show their friends in Rome. With their very expensive shoes (one thousand dollars a pair in the least) they will trample on the ground coffee, maybe they will even spend a tear to replace their former «Good, Americans-got-it-good», and guess what they'll do afterwards. They will go to buy the gas-masks in sale for those who fear a chemical or a biological attack. Is it not chic to go back Rome with a gas-mask bought here? It permits to boast: «Gee! I risked my life in New York!». It also permits to start a new fashion, the fashion of the Dangerous Holidays. First they invented the Intelligent Holidays, they who do not have a single drop of intelligence, now they'll invent the Dangerous Holidays. They who do not have a single drop of courage. And no need to say that the de luxe cicadas of the other European countries will do exactly the same. Here finally is what I think of them too.

* * *

Dear English, French, Belgians, Dutch, Germans, Austrians, Hungarians, Scandinavians, Spanish, Portuguese, Greeks, etcetera amen. Don't do like that Prime Minister who gloated as a happy bride before knowing what I would say about him. Don't jump with joy for the burning reproaches I launch against the Italies that are not my Italy. Your countries are no better than mine. Ten out of ten cases they are dismaying copies of mine, and almost everything I said against the Italians goes also for you who are made from the same mold. Oh, yes, dearest: in that sense we really belong to a great family. Identical the faults, the cowardices, the hypocrisies. Identical the blindness, the deafness, the lack of wisdom, the masochism. Identical the licentiousness smuggled as liberty, as freedom. Identical the ignorance and the lack of leadership that favors the Moslem invasion. Identical the fad of the Politically Correct that encourages it. To believe me you only have to observe the Financial Club you proudly call European Union. A club that only serves to impose the rhetorical nonsense called Common Currency, to compete or pretend to compete with America, to pay fabulous and undeserved salaries (tax free) to the members of its inept and useless Parliament. And to bother me with its populist imbecilities. For instance, the one that wants to abolish seventy canine races. (All-dogs-must-be-equal, as the anthropologist Ida Magli has ironically commented). Or the one that wants to standardize the seats of the European planes. (All-asses-must-be-equal, I add). A club that only speaks English or French, never Italian or Spanish or Flemish or Finnish or Norwegian etcetera, and where the centenary troika England-France-Germany still commands. A club that shelters more than fifteen million sons of Allah and God knows how many of their terrorists or candidate terrorists or future terrorists. A club that fornicates like a whore with the Arab countries and fills its pockets with their filthy petrodollars. The same petrodollars with which the Saudi Uncle Scrooges buy our ancient palaces, our banks, our commercial and industrial firms. A club, moreover, that dares to speak of «Cultural Similarities with the Middle East». (What the hell does it mean Cultural-Similarities-with-the-Middle-East, you chatterers, you mentally retarded?!? Where the hell is the cultural similarity with the Middle East, you cretins, you silly clowns?!? At Mecca? At Bethlehem, at Gaza, at Damascus, at Beirut?!? At Cairo, at Tripoli, at Nairobi, at Tehran, at Baghdad, at Kabul?!?).

When I was very young, about seventeen or so, I longed so much for a united Europe! I came from a war in which the Italians and the French, the Italians and the English, the Italians and the Greeks, the Italians and the Finns, the Italians and the Russians, the Italians and the Germans, the Germans and the French and the English and the Poles and the Dutch and the Danes and the Finns and the Russians etcetera had pitilessly slaughtered each other: remember? The damned Second World War. Plunged up to his neck in the brandnew struggle, my father preached the European

183

Federalism. The great mirage of Carlo and Nello Rosselli. He held rallies, he spoke to the crowds, he chanted: «Europe, Europe! We must make Europe!». And full of enthusiasm, of joyous trust, I followed him as I had done in the days when he bravely chanted Liberty-Liberty. Along with a never tasted peace I began to know those who only a few years before had been my foes, and seeing the Germans without uniforms, without machine-guns, without cannons, I thought: «They are like us, my God. They dress like us, they eat like us, they laugh like us, they love music and poetry and art, beauty, like us. They pray or do not pray like me... How is it possible, then, that they harmed me so much, that they terrorized and persecuted and killed us so much?». Then I thought: «But we harmed them too, we killed them too!». And with a shudder of horror I wondered whether in one way or another, during the Resistance, I too had contributed to the death of some German. If I too had killed one of them. I wondered, yes. And while answering myself «may-be-yes, surely-yes», I felt a sort of shame. I felt as if I had fought in the Middle Ages, when Florence and nearby Siena waged war on each other, and the silvery waters of the Arno River became all red with blood. The blood of the Florentines and the blood of the Sienese. With a shudder of incredulity I disputed my pride of having been a soldier for my country, for my patria, and I sighed: «Enough, enough! Father is right! Europe, Europe! We must unite, we must make Europe!». Well... the Italians of the Italies which are not my Italy say that we have made Europe. And the Germans, the French, the English, the Spanish, the Dutch etcetera, I mean the Great Family's members who resemble those Italians, repeat it with them. But this frustrating and disappointing and insignificant Financial Club which bothers me with its Common Currency, its populist imbecilities, its sons of Allah who want to erase my civilization, this European Union which chatters of Cultural-Similarities-with-the-Middle-East and meanwhile ignores my beautiful language, meanwhile sacrifices my national identity, is not the Europe I dreamed of when my father chanted Europe-Europe. It is not Europe. It is the suicide of Europe.

* * *

What is my Europe, then, what is my Italy? Listen: in the case of Europe, I really do not know. I cannot know. The real unity of Europe is inevitably poisoned by the difference of our many languages, by the discomforts and the suspicions that ensue from it, by the old rivalries and rancours rooted inside our tormented past of fratricidal wars. And the hope of overcoming these obstacles belongs to the realm of my adolescence's fantasies, utopias. I mean to the time when, tasting a never tasted peace and looking at the Germans without uniforms, without machine-guns, without cannons, I felt as if I had fought in the Middle Ages. As if I had contributed to make the silvery waters of the Arno River red with blood. The blood of the Florentines and of the Sienese... But in the case of Italy, I know. And I say: simple, my dear, simple. It is the Italy opposed to the ones about which I have been speaking until now: an ideal Italy. An Italy not tyrannized by the sons of Allah and by the parasites, the cicadas. An Italy that loves her flag and places the right hand over her heart to salute it. The Italy I dreamed when I was a little girl without decent shoes. And this Italy, an Italy that exists, that is always silenced or ridiculed or insulted yet exists, woe betide those who want to steal it from me. Woe betide those who invade it. Whoever the invaders are. Because whether they be the French of Napoleon or the Austrians of Franz Joseph or the Germans of Hitler or the Moslems of Ousama Bin Laden, for me it is exactly the same. Whether they come with troops and cannons or with children and boats, idem.

Now, stop. I have said what I had to say. My rage and my pride ordered me to do so. My clean conscience and my age permitted me to obey that order, that duty. But now the duty is fulfilled. Thus, stop. Enough. Stop.

ORIANA FALLACI

New York, September 2001
Florence, September 2002

Printed in Italy by
Nuovo Istituto Italiano d'Arti Grafiche - Bergamo
January 2007